Augustus Woodbury

A Narrative of the Campaign of the First Rhode Island Regiment, in the Spring and Summer of 1861

Illustrated with a portrait and map

Augustus Woodbury

A Narrative of the Campaign of the First Rhode Island Regiment, in the Spring and Summer of 1861
Illustrated with a portrait and map

ISBN/EAN: 9783337373634

Printed in Europe, USA, Canada, Australia, Japan

Cover: Foto ©ninafisch / pixelio.de

More available books at **www.hansebooks.com**

A NARRATIVE

OF

THE CAMPAIGN

OF THE

First Rhode Island Regiment,

IN THE SPRING AND SUMMER OF 1861.

ILLUSTRATED WITH A PORTRAIT AND MAP.

BY AUGUSTUS WOODBURY,

CHAPLAIN OF THE REGIMENT.

PROVIDENCE:
SIDNEY S. RIDER
1862.

Entered according to Act of Congress, in the year 1862, by

AUGUSTUS WOODBURY,

in the Clerk's Office of the District Court of Rhode Island.

KNOWLES, ANTHONY & CO., PRINTERS,
PROVIDENCE.

I DEDICATE THIS BOOK TO

Major General AMBROSE E. BURNSIDE,

OUR BELOVED COMMANDER;

TO THE

OFFICERS AND MEMBERS OF OUR REGIMENT,

AT HOME AND ABROAD;

AND TO THE

Memory **of** our Noble Dead.

PREFATORY NOTE.

In the little volume, which I give to the public, I have aimed simply to write a familiar and faithful account of the campaign of the First Regiment Rhode Island Detached Militia. In the compilation of the Appendix, I desire to express my obligations to Adjutant General MAURAN and his assistants, for ready access to the muster rolls and other documents pertaining to the Rhode Island Regiments now in the field; and to the many friends in Newport, Pawtucket, Westerly, Woonsocket and Providence, who have kindly assisted me in obtaining information respecting the members of our Regiment that have again entered the service of the country.

CONTENTS.

I. FORMATION AND DEPARTURE OF THE REGIMENT 1
II. MARCH TO WASHINGTON AND ARRIVAL AT THAT CITY 18
III. CAMP LIFE 30
IV. EXPEDITION TOWARDS HARPER'S FERRY 56
V. CAMP LIFE RESUMED . . . 68
VI. BATTLE OF BULL RUN . . . 74
VII. CONCLUSION 108

* APPENDIX
    A.—THE THREE MONTHS' VOLUNTEERS 117
    B.—THE SEA GULL AND HER CARGO . 151
    C.—THE DEAD 151
    D.—ROLL OF THE REGIMENT . . 169
    E.—FINAL PARADE . . . 232
    F.—THE REGIMENTAL FLAGS . 239
    G.—MISCELLANEOUS . 248
ADDENDA 259

CAMPAIGN
O
FIRST R~~~~~~~~.

I.

FORMATION AND DEPARTURE.

When the first of April, 1861, dawned upon the people of the United States, it found them in a feverish and excited condition. Seven States had already declared themselves independent of the Government of the Union, and had combined to form a provisional government. It was very well understood, that four more were only waiting for a pretext to engage in the same revolutionary action. The property of the Government, in localities favorable to the insurgents, had been seized and appropriated to the use of the rebellious States. A president of the United States had been inaugurated amid circumstances of extraordinary peril; and it was matter of doubt in the minds of many, whether he and the cabinet which he formed had sufficient firmness, courage, patriotism and good sense, to guide the ship of State out from the midst of the breakers among which she had unhappily been driven.

But the interest of the nation centred at a small fort in the harbor of Charleston, South Carolina, garrisoned by less than a hundred men. It was known that this little fortification, over whose ramparts still floated, defiantly to all sedition and rebellion, the Stars and Stripes, was surrounded by batteries ready to open fire upon its devoted walls. Would Sumter be re-inforced? Would it be supplied with provisions? Would it be evacuated? The administration determined to throw supplies into the fort, if possible, and, at the same time, to re-inforce Fort Pickens, in the harbor of Pensacola, which had not yet been seized. Notice of the intention to do the first was served upon the government of the State of South Carolina. It was the signal for the commencement of hostilities. On Friday, April 12th, the bombardment of Fort Sumter began. For more than thirty hours, the brave Anderson, with his company of soldiers, sustained the assault. At last, human strength could endure no longer, and, on Saturday, April 13th, the flag of the United States was lowered before the overwhelming forces of rebels in arms. The intelligence was flashed through the country. It was like the fiery cross hurrying through the clans of Scotland. The Southern press boldly avowed the intention of the rebels to seize the capital of the nation. President Lincoln issued his proclamation for seventy-five thousand volunteers to defend the city of Washington.* He called upon Congress to meet. He bade the rebellious forces of the South to lay down their arms and disperse. It was like the peal of a trumpet. The people of the North rushed to arms. By Wednesday, Pennsylvania, New York, Massachusetts, had their men ready for departure. On Thursday, the Sixth Massachusetts Regiment marched down Broadway, and on Friday, after consecrating anew the 19th of April, by dyeing the streets of Baltimore with the blood of Massachusetts patriots, the regiment entered the Capital. The

---

* See Appendix A.

Seventh New York and the Eighth Massachusetts followed as far as Perryville. But there, information was received that the bridges between that place and Baltimore had been destroyed; and, taking possession of a steamer, they proceeded to Annapolis.

Meanwhile the State of Rhode Island had not been idle. Governor Sprague, in common with the authorities of other loyal States, had already, with commendable promptness, offered the services of the State militia to the president.* Immediately after the reception of Mr. Lincoln's proclamation, the General Assembly was convened. A liberal bounty was voted, and provision was made by the generosity of the authorities for the enlist-

---

* This offer of troops was made to Mr. Buchanan, who saw fit to reject it. It was afterwards made to Mr. Lincoln. On the 12th of January, 1861, Secretary Bartlett wrote to the Secretary of War, that Rhode Island would do its utmost to assist the Government. January 15th, Col. William Goddard, of the Governor's staff, reached Washington, with the tender of 1000 men and a battery of light artillery, and was favorably received by Gen. Scott. January 11th, the legislature of the State of New York voted to tender the whole military power of the State to the president. January 18th, the legislature of Massachusetts passed a similar vote. January 16th, Maj. Gen. Sandford, of New York city, tendered a division of 7000 men.

ment of a regiment of infantry and a battery
of light artillery. Ambrose E. Burnside, Esq.,
then treasurer of the Illinois Central Railroad
Co., and residing in the city of New York,
was appointed Colonel of the First Regiment,
which was to proceed immediately to the
scene of action ; and, under his direction, its
equipment rapidly proceeded. It was a
memorable week for our city and our State.
The streets of Providence resounded with the
tramp of armed men and the notes of martial
music. The vestries of the churches, halls,
private dwellings, were filled with women at
work upon the outfit of the soldiers. Two
thousand five hundred men volunteered for
the defence of the Government. The villages
vied with the cities, and each community furnished its representatives for the maintenance
of their country's institutions. Young men,
buoyant with hope ; middle-aged men, who
felt the fire of patriotism kindling their hearts;
men, who had passed the time allotted by law
for the period of military service,—were alike
moved, as by one common impulse, and sought
to find a place where they could do something
for the common weal. Men of all ranks and

conditions stood side by side in this great movement. The young millionaire, who had never been taught or accustomed to perform a single labor for himself; the darling of fortune, with the tastes of a Sybarite and the pride of a gentleman; the student from college shades and the seclusion of the scholar's cloister; the thrifty mechanic, whose daily toil was cheered by the affections that brightened his humble home; the laborer, bronzed by his daily tasks; the exile from beyond the sea, who had seen service on the battle-fields of Europe, and wore the honorable scars of a soldier who had fought for freedom,—all were there, eager for the opportunities of duty, and ready to imperil life, fortune—everything but honor—in the cause of liberty and law. It seemed as though both the artificial and the natural distinctions of society had been, for the time, abrogated, and the barriers broken down in the hour of the nation's emergency. The inborn humanity of us all stood manifest to the day. Class, caste, sect, party, were all forgotten. Rich and poor, native and foreigner, Protestant and Catholic, Radical and Conservative, Republican and Democrat, alike felt the mighty impulse. Before this fresh gale of loyalty, the prejudices of men were scattered and swept away as mists before the morning breeze.

Of the numerous body of men that presented themselves for the service of their country, twelve hundred were selected to compose the battery of artillery and the regiment of infantry. that had been offered to the Government. The battery, under command of Captain C. H. Tompkins, and accompanied by the Lieutenant Governor elect, Hon. Samuel G. Arnold, left Providence on Thursday, April 18th, for Easton, Pennsylvania, in order to perfect its recruits in drill before entering upon the active service that was anticipated. On Saturday, April 20th, the first detachment of the regiment of infantry, a detail from ten companies, numbering five hundred and forty-four officers and men, accompanied by the Governor, and Cols. Lyman B. Frieze and William Goddard, of his personal staff, departed for the seat of war.*

---

* By the provisions of the law, under which the First Regiment was detached, and sent to Washington, the Governor of

The regiment of infantry was composed of ten companies, from the following cities and towns, viz. :—Providence, Newport, Pawtucket, Westerly and Woonsocket. Providence furnished six companies, viz. :—" First Light Infantry," two, C and D; "Mechanics Rifles," two, G and H; "National Cadets," one, A; "Artillery," one, B. Newport furnished one company; "Artillery," F. Pawtucket, one, " Light Guard," E. Westerly, one, " Rifles," I ; and Woonsocket, one, " Guards," K. The relative rank of the company officers was determined by lot, in Providence, as follows, viz. :—1. Capt. Arthur F. Dexter, Co. A, with its post on the right flank; 2. Capt. Nathaniel W. Brown, Co. D, on the left flank; 3. Captain George W Tew, Co. F, color company, in the centre; 4. Capt. William W Brown, Co. C, third in line ; 5. Capt. Nicholas Van Slyck, Co. B, seventh in line ; 6. Capt. Stephen R. Bucklin, Co. E, second in line; 7 Capt. Charles

---

the State was placed in command of the troops, till they should be mustered into the service of the United States, when, of course, his authority ceased. Gov. Sprague's counsel, however, was frequently sought by Col. Burnside, and was always cheerfully given.

W H. Day, Co. H, ninth in line; 8. Capt. Peter Simpson, Co. K, sixth in line ; 9. Capt. Henry C. Card, Co. I, fourth in line ; 10. Capt. John T. Pitman, Co. G,* eighth in line. The battery was the Providence Marine Corps of Artillery,† recruited to its complete strength. It is a curious and significant fact, that the names of several of the officers of this regiment are identical with those of the officers in the early regiments of the Revolution. Among the officers of independent companies, elected June, 1775, are those bearing the

---

* Capt. David A. Peloubet went out in command of Co. G, but was detached at Annapolis.

† The caissons, battery wagons, and the different *materiel* belonging to this company, had been put in complete order, during the winter of 1860–61, chiefly through the exertions of Mr. George H. Smith, Quartermaster of the company. It was mainly owing to Mr. Smith's indefatigable labors, that the Marine Corps of Artillery was ready to move at the short notice which it received. The caissons, forges, guns, &c., passed through the summer campaign; were transferred to Capt. Reynolds' company after the Battle of Bull Run ; were engaged at Poolesville, Harper's Ferry, Bolivar and vicinity, during the following winter; and were used in Gen. McClellan's advance to Richmond, in the spring and summer of 1862. This severe usage they have borne, with scarcely a necessity for repair, so thoroughly was the labor performed before they left Rhode Island.

names of Pitman, Warner, Wheaton, Bucklin, Tower, Harris, Knight and Allen. Upon the list of officers of a regiment raised January, 1776, are the names of Dexter, Tew, Slocum, Sprague, Reynolds and Carr. There was a Colonel Nathaniel Brown among the Revolutionary officers, who was represented by the Captain of Company D, now Colonel of the Third Regiment of Rhode Island Heavy Artillery, at Port Royal, S. C. There was also a Lieutenant Zephaniah Brown, who, in our regiment, found a representative in the Second Lieutenant of Company C—an officer that added fresh honor to his ancestry and name. Thus, the spirit of the heroes of the Revolution lived again in their descendants. The valor of those was needed to found an empire of freemen; the valor of these to preserve it. Both went forth from their homes at the sacred call of duty. Animated by the same deep love of country, the sons proved themselves worthy of their sires.

It seemed as though almost the entire population of the State of Rhode Island crowded the streets of Providence, to witness the departure of this gallant band of soldiers, and to bid them God-speed upon their dangerous enterprise. The wharves, the heights upon the shores of the harbor, and the coasts of Narragansett Bay, were covered with spectators. Cannon belched forth its thunder. Cheers of men rent the air. The prayers and blessings of tearful women consecrated the hour. As the steamer, in which the command had embarked, left the bay, and entered upon the waters beyond, the boom of the heavy columbiads upon the parapet of Fort Adams announced to those upon the sea and those upon the land, that the shores of Rhode Island had been left, perhaps forever, by the flower of her youth and the prime of her manhood. The sun went down in splendor; the moon cast her silvery sheen across the waters; prayers were breathed from devout hearts, and the stillness of night reigned through the crowded vessel.

Sunday was spent on board the transport, in the harbor of New York. The great city had reached the climax of enthusiasm. The flag of the United States was floating from every prominent point. The spires of the churches bore the Stars and Stripes only below the cross, and the pulpits were draped with the national banner. It was known that several New York and Massachusetts regiments were preparing for embarkation. Four or five ocean steamers were taking on board their supplies for a voyage to Washington As soon as they were ready, they were to sail under convoy of the Harriet Lane. The fleet got under way late in the afternoon. The Rhode Islanders, transferred to the steamer Coatzacoalcos, soon followed. Heaven seemed to smile propitiously upon our expedition The south wind breathed softly across the sea The sun rose and set in a cloudless sky. The watchful stars looked down upon us in peace The white sails of homeward bound ships approaching a land convulsed with civil war, and of those outward bound, carrying to the nations the unwelcome tidings of our intestine strife, gleamed across the waters.

During the afternoon of Monday, a little tug came dancing over the billows, bearing the flag of the Union. She came up under our quarter, spoke us, communicated the intelligence of the destruction of our navy yard at Norfolk, by our own government, then steamed away again for New York. Before the close of day, we came in sight of the capes of Virginia. At nightfall, we were within Lynn Haven Roads. But, as the shadows deepened, we looked in vain for the beacon lights by which the skilful sailor lays his course. They had been extinguished or misplaced, and at any time we might be among the breakers or exposed to capture by the forces of an enemy. It was useless to proceed farther, and the ship soon swung idly at her anchors.

As can easily be imagined, the night was anxiously spent by those who were, at the best, but novices in warfare. A hostile shore was but a few miles distant on either side. The rebel government had issued letters of marque. There were but one or two war vessels, belonging to our own government, in this vicinity, and the alarm indicated by the recent destruction of the neighboring navy yard, might embolden the foe to the performance of desperate deeds. What could prevent the destruction of the whole fleet of transports by a sudden attack of armed boats from the Virginia shore? Might not the guns of Fortress Monroe be avoided by some bold privateer? Indeed, did we still possess the fortress? Every precaution was taken against surprise. Ammunition was liberally distributed to the troops. The trustiest and most faithful men were stationed as guards, upon the most exposed parts of the ship, and those who were off duty lay with their arms by their sides. But nature asserted her power, and the tramp of the sentinels upon the hurricane deck soon became indistinct, and was lost as grateful sleep closed our eyes.

The next day dawned bright and beautiful as its predecessors. There had been no alarm during the night, and, at an early hour, the ship proceeded on her way. There, at last, are the stone walls of the fortress. There is the flag-staff. Thank God! there is the glorious old flag still flying from its head! And there also is a Massachusetts regiment to reinforce its garrison,—the old Bay State always ahead. The sloop-of-war Cumberland lay there, too, and the Baltic, which had arrived before dark the day previous, with her decks crowded with a thousand men and more, who were to be our companions on the march and in the field. A boat or two, with naval officers on board, went from ship to ship with measured oars. The Harriet Lane came in sight to windward, with our consorts. We received our orders for Annapolis, and were soon steaming on the way. Up Chesapeake Bay, through the hours of that genial day, we sailed—four large vessels filled with soldiers, and the trim and graceful little cutter leading the van. Occasional snatches of song, cheers, and friendly hails were sent from vessel to vessel; bayonets and arms glistened in the sunlight as the men were mustered upon deck and drilled in preparation for their expected service; the shores of Maryland, houses, trees, vessels, loomed up in strange mirage, in constantly varying forms. The day wore on in social, pleasant chat, not unmingled with serious words, as we thought of the mission upon which we had been sent.

The twilight of Tuesday found us entering Annapolis Roads, and the fleet was anchored in the close vicinity of our convoy and the frigate Constitution. The next day was passed in comparative idleness. We went up to the harbor of the Maryland city, and prepared to go on shore. But owing to the unavoidable delay, incident to all military movements, and a smart shower of rain, which was opportune for our next day's march, but vastly inconvenient for our present disembarkation, we did not land the troops until an hour in the afternoon too late for any further progress. We found the town in possession of our forces, with General Butler, of Massachusetts, in command. But the only place from which our flag could be seen, was that occupied by the United States Naval Academy. The Seventh New York had been there, but had gone, on the day before, with the Eighth Massachusetts. Wonderful stories were told of the conduct of the troops—how some of the Massachusetts men had found a disabled locomotive which they themselves had manufactured in more peaceful times, in some machine shop at Lowell or Lawrence, and now repaired it; how the Marblehead men, with their maritime experience, had gone to the help of the cadets of the Naval School, and had succeeded in getting the Constitution over the bar; how the two regiments had gone away together—the dainty gentlemen of New York with the hardy mechanics of Essex county—to repair the railroad which disloyal hands had attempted to destroy, or to fight their way through to Washington, if necessary. Then came rumors of a skirmish on the road, and some credulous individual had even heard of two or three of the wounded men that had been brought back. Then again, a crossing had been made on the lower Potomac, and some Southern general was marching through the State of Maryland, to cut off the communications of Washington with the North. We paid but little attention to these rumors, and prepared to pass the night in quiet. We were most kindly received by the officers of the Naval School, and several unoccupied buildings were placed at our disposal. That night, we had our first experience of sleeping on the soft side of a hard pine floor.

2*

II.

MARCH TO WASHINGTON AND ARRIVAL AT THAT CITY

THURSDAY morning, the regiment was earl[y] astir. Most of our baggage and stores wer[e] left on board the transport, to be afterward[s] conveyed to Washington. Sundry broke[n] down horses and mules, with a few ricket[y] carts, were procured at fabulous prices t[o] carry the remainder which could not be take[n] with our own teams, and we got off upon th[e] road at five o'clock. The Seventy-first Ne[w] York preceded us about an hour. The da[y] was clear and bracing, and the march wa[s] really a delightful experience. No enem[y] appeared to oppose our progress, and the da[y] passed without adventure. But not, howeve[r,] without accident. Private William Gallaghe[r,] belonging to Company A, fell from a fenc[e] during a temporary halt, and broke one of hi[s] legs. He continued to be an invalid durin[g] our whole term of service. But the genuin[e] bravery, with which he bore the pain and confinement, is worthy of all praise.

The country through which we marched was almost entirely deserted. Occasionally, a horseman would pass us on the road, whose dark and scowling looks betokened that, at least, he was no friend to the soldiers who occupied the highway, or to the cause in which they were engaged. At times, indeed, our salutations were returned with an air, in which a wish not to be outdone in politeness by the " vulgar Yankees," and a secret though hearty execration upon our enterprise, were curiously mingled. Again, we were told that we never should reach Washington alive, and the wish was manifestly " father to the thought." From one or two houses, only, were we greeted with any show of cordiality. Thus we plodded our way along, overtaking the Seventy-first about noon, at a place some seven or eight miles from Annapolis, where they had halted for rest. An hour or two of repose freshened the men again, and the march was resumed,—this time with the Rhode Island regiment in advance. Another halt was made at a late hour in the afternoon, when we pushed on once more for a suitable locality for passing the night. The place selected for our bivouac was reached by the head of the column about eight o'clock in the evening. The rear guard, with the baggage, came up two hours later. But for the last few hours, suspicious signs had been observed upon the heights that bordered the road. Columns of smoke had been seen rising from different points, as though signal fires were lighted as we passed. But no attack was made, and the regiment passed the night in safety.

Upon this day's march the duties of the rear guard, Co. I, of Westerly, were excessively onerous. For the last seven or eight miles, the roads were in extremely bad condition, being narrow, sandy and difficult for men and horses. The wagons brought from Providence, and the miserable carts purchased at Annapolis, were not sufficiently strong for the transportation of heavy stores, and the march was delayed, from time to time, by the breaking of harnesses, and the refractory conduct of horses and mules. But the perseverance and energy of our men overcame every obstacle, and their efforts were rewarded by a well-earned success. Col. Burnside, in his report to the Governor, pays the following merited compliment to the rear guard :—

"It gives me the utmost pleasure to express the great satisfaction which I feel, respecting the vigilance and fidelity with which Capt. Card and his company performed the hazardous and difficult duty incident to their position in the column of march. To. Col. William Goddard was assigned the direction of the baggage-train, and the admirable manner in which this responsible post was filled deserves the highest commendation."

The scene of the bivouac, as it then appeared, was highly picturesque. An open field, a few acres in extent, lay upon the side of the road, protected in the rear by a dense wood and having the railroad in front. A house stood near, a sort of cross between a corner grocery, a grog-shop, a tavern, a railroad station and a farm-house, but an undoubted rendezvous of secessionists, several of whom collected during the night. Our force, good equipment and vigilance forbade any attempt upon us, even if it had been devised. As this was the point at which we had been told that an attack would be made, and as here we were informed that there were several hundred armed men a mile or two distant, who only awaited an opportunity to assail an inferior force, the utmost precaution was deemed necessary. Sentinels were stationed in the woods, along the railroad track, and around the house, which was now occupied by the Governor, the staff officers and the sick and disabled men. The ground of the bivouac was held by the different companies in proper order; camp fires were lighted, and the men were grouped around them, wrapped in their red blankets and with their muskets within ready grasp. The moon, just past her full, poured down a flood of soft light; the whippoorwill from the neighboring forest sent forth her plaintive note; the sentinels slowly paced to and fro by the roadside and among the trees; the camp fires burnt brightly, and when, in the night, the Seventy-first marched by, and a portion of a Massachusetts regiment passed in the railroad train which had been extemporized for the occasion, they described the scene as strikingly impressive and beautiful. Three o'clock in the morning, was the hour appointed for our departure, and at that time every man was awake. Provisions had been served to the men the evening previous, and I have lively recollections of some excellent hot roasted potatoes and salt, enjoyed near the camp fire of Company C, about midnight, and a most villainous breakfast in the neighboring house an hour or two later. To every question, on the day previous, as to the distance to our destination—the Junction of the Annapolis Branch and Baltimore and Ohio Railroads— the invariable answer was, "nine miles," and the poet of the Seventy-first afterwards improved the occasion. We supposed, therefore, that we had a long march before us. We found we had been deceived, and after a short hour's march, upon a road leading through deserted plantations, we reached the railroad station. We found the Junction in the possession of the Seventy-first, and the almost ubiquitous Massachusetts troops. By ten o'clock, the regiment, with its baggage, was placed upon and in the cars, and, two hours later, we were in Washington, finding quarters at the Patent Office. The Seventh New

York had reached there the day before; part of the Eighth Massachusetts that had been guarding the railroad, were on the train with us, and we, with them, were welcomed with every expression of delight by the loyal citizens of the Capital.

Washington was like a beleaguered city. For nearly a week, all communication with the North had been cut off. Since the arrival of the Sixth Massachusetts, on Friday, the 19th, up to the arrival of the Seventh New York, and Eighth Massachusetts, on Thursday, the 25th, nothing whatever had been known of the doings of the loyal States. How the President's proclamation had been received, and what response the people were disposed to give to it, were matters only of conjecture. A hostile city, held in subjection by the terrors of a mob, lay between the capital and the free States. It was feared that the scenes of the 19th would be re-enacted, on the occasion of the passage of every regiment through its streets. It was soon known that there was no approach to Baltimore, and the citizens of Washington were daily expecting to hear the roar of hostile cannon planted on the heights of Arlington. The regiments from Annapolis brought the cheering intelligence of the prompt and opportune action of General Butler, and the officers of the Government breathed more freely. The arrival of the First Detachment, followed in a few days by that of the Second Detachment of the First Rhode-Island Regiment and the Light Artillery, which had come up the Potomac, with the subsequent daily inflowing of additional forces, placed the safety of the capital beyond a doubt.

But it can well be imagined, with what feelings of satisfaction the arrival of troops like ours would be hailed. We were well equipped. We had our ammunition, our baggage wagons, provisions for two or three weeks with us, and, fully officered, we were ready to take the field, if necessary, at an hour's notice.

The State authorities had wisely determined to place in the capital, at the earliest possible moment, a body of men who could be immediately effective. Every provision had been made for every emergency. If we were sent to a beleaguered city, it had been decided that we should go with the least possible embarassment to the general Government. The regiment was made up of picked men. Ample supplies had been furnished. The Commander-in-chief of our State was with us, and was received with cordial attentions. The Administration gratefully appreciated such decisive and complete action, and at once placed its most commodious building at our disposal.

The acquisition to the cause of a man like Col. Burnside, with his military education, his long experience and his well-tried bravery upon distant fields, was of a value beyond calculation. The First Rhode Island Regiment, therefore, early gained a high place in the respect and affections of the people and authorities at Washington. The State was indeed small, but she had promptly and nobly responded to the call of the chief magistrate of the nation, and had now sent forth her choicest sons, under the command of as noble and gallant a soldier as could be found within the borders of the republic.

The curiosities of the Patent Office afforde our men ample materials for study, whic were not suffered to remain unimproved. Here were models of all kinds of machines.

which our mechanics viewed with perpetual interest. Here were articles of value from beyond the sea, the gifts of foreign princes to our own rulers. Here, also, were the relics of heroic times,—the original Declaration of Independence ; the staff of Franklin ; the sword, the uniform and the camp chest of Washington. The Library furnished reading matter for the student, and the Census Office gave to the statistician abundant encouragement for the hope of the future greatness of the republic. Here a soldier would find the model of a machine which had been invented by some member of his own family—perhaps by himself. There he would be intently studying some new arrangement of mechanical forces, which would be suggestive of subsequent investigation. Other public buildings would attract the attention of our men, in their hours of leisure, and the Professors at the Smithsonian Institution were surprised to find, that, among the privates of our regiment, there were those who could creditably hold their own in discussions upon matters of science, history and art. Our life in Washington had thus commenced under the most favorable auspices, and our campaign promised to be a profitable experience rather than a dangerous enterprise.

On the second day of May, the regiment was mustered into the service of the United States, for the period of three months. The ceremony was performed in the grounds of the Capitol, at the close of a bright spring day, and was witnessed by a large number of spectators. Eleven hundred men were drawn up on three sides of a square, and as their voices rose in full response,—not one refusing then to take the oath of loyalty,—swearing to bear true allegiance to the Government of the United States, and to oppose all its enemies, the hour was solemnized forever in memory. We marched back to our quarters, feeling a new sense of our responsibility, for now the whole country had a right to expect brave deeds of us, and we had called God to witness our vows of fidelity and obedience. The ceremony was performed in the most impressive manner, by Major Irvin McDowell, assisted by General G. R. Thomas. The oath of allegiance was as follows:— "I—— ——, do solemnly swear that I will bear true allegiance to the United States of America, and that I will serve honestly and faithfully against all their enemies and opposers whatsoever, and observe and obey the orders of the President of the United States, and the orders of the officers appointed over me, according to the rules and regulations for the government of the armies of the United States: so help me God!"

On this day, the Battery of Artillery arrived, and on the 7th of May, the officers and men were mustered into the service of the United States.

III.

CAMP LIFE.

For the next week or two, the regiment was preparing to go into camp. A site had been selected on the slope of a hill, about a mile to the north of the Capitol, and near the road leading to Bladensburg. The environs of Washington are eminently beautiful, and the position of our camp, in this respect, was unsurpassed. Arlington Heights, then free from fortifications; Georgetown Heights, and the elevated land upon the south and east of the city were in full view; the silvery Potomac gleamed in the distance, while immediately below and in front lay the city itself, with its unfinished public buildings and its clustered dwellings, to which distance lent an enchantment which they themselves did not possess. Upon the brow of the hill, our artillery was planted; a slight depression of the spacious lawn, forming an amphitheatre, was our parade ground; a grove of trees occupied our rear, and the dwelling house of the proprietor of the estate furnished us with the most ample and the most comfortable hospital arrangements. Our regiment provided its own mechanics, and in two weeks' time a miniature village, for the accommodation of twelve hundred inhabitants, was built.* Rough board huts, with sleeping arrangements for eighteen persons each, and with a porch in front for the dining hall, were our habitations. Our streets received the names of those familiar at home, and our village was named for the Governor of the State. Our tables were resplendent with the richest plate that the tin manufactories of the country could produce, and groaned beneath those numerous luxuries with which the army regulations tickle the palate and tempt the appetite. Beds of straw invited to sweet repose,—and if we chose to sleep in our boots it was no-

---

* The camp was planned by Henry A. De Witt, then private in Company C, but afterwards promoted to Lieutenant of Engineers; and the huts were built under the superintendence of Col. Goddard and Lieutenant William R. Walker, of Company E.

body's business but our own. Many of the squads—"messes" as we called them in camp—took great pride in the embellishment of their huts; and flowers, books, hangings of variegated cambric of patriotic colors, and musical instruments were not uncommon. A little cellar occupied the centre of the hut, and served as a refrigerator, well supplied with ice by the generosity of our friends at home.[*]

Occasionally, one could find a table spread with crockery or delf, and boasting a cloth, or a floor covered with straw matting. But these instances of comfort were rare. We had left such enervating things as carpets, couches, easy chairs, bedsteads and the like, in the realm of civilization which was now far away, and they existed for us only in our memories and dreams. We were proving to ourselves, how unnecessary were many of those things which we had been accustomed to consider as especially needful for us, and how small were really the requirements of life. Approaching the condition of primeval man,

---

[*] See Appendix B.

we were living in a Paradise; but alas! without an Eve.

The commissariat was under the charge of a noted caterer of our own State, whose rotundity of person was a good evidence of his skill in cookery. He had under his charge a detachment of cooks, who were engaged from morning till night in the performance of their necessary duties. The soldier is always a hungry man, and the patience, as well as the industry, of those whose business it was to keep him well fed, was sometimes put to severe tests. When our two regiments were encamped together, the office of the Commissary was by no means a sinecure. Nine hundred and sixty gallons of coffee barely sufficed for the morning and evening draught. Our substantial brick bakery, built upon the camp ground, received daily into its insatiate maw, from eight to ten barrels of flour and thirteen hundred pounds of meat. One hundred and eighty pans of gingerbread would sometimes, of an evening, smoke upon our supper tables, flanked by delicious strawberries, cherries and other fruit, which in their season were daily for sale within the camp.

A substantial dish of pork and beans—one and a half barrels of the former and three barrels of the latter—would weekly remind us of New England institutions. One barrel of pork, three barrels of beef, and three hundred and twenty-five cabbages, were the ingredients of an occasional "boiled dish." During the week preceding the battle of Bull Run, there were cooked at our camp in Washington, and sent to Centreville, three thousand pounds of fresh meat, twenty barrels of beef and a wagon load of bread. The beef and bread were sent out on Saturday, and fell into the hands of the rebels, with other supplies, which, I have no doubt, were duly appreciated. In the season of whortleberries, one mammoth pudding attested the skill of the manager of our *cuisine*. The recipe may not be found in the "Cookery Books," the "Housekeeper's Companion," and the "Domestic Economy" of our lady friends, and perhaps might be a puzzle to that celebrated gastronomer, Dr. Kitchiner himself. I give it, therefore, for the benefit of my young friends who are beginning life, and of all whom it may otherwise concern :—Take one hundred and eighty quarts of berries, eight bushels of Indian meal, one-half barrel of flour, twenty dozens of eggs and forty gallons of milk. Stir well together, and add (of course) " spice to the taste."

Life in camp varied but little from day to day. At sunrise, or at five o'clock, the "reveille" was beat, when every private must attend the roll call of his company, in whatever garb he chose,—and the garbs were various. Then, in the warm days of summer, there were company drills before breakfast. At six or half past six, was the summons to breakfast, called by a singular inconsequence of nomenclature, " Peas upon a trencher," for the very obvious reason that there were no peas and no trencher. At eight o'clock, the guards were posted. After that, when the weather permitted, there were more company drills of an hour or two. At one in the afternoon, " roast beef" was beaten. Battalion drills occupied the coolest part of the afternoon, and at sunset the daily dress parade closed the ordinary duties of the soldier's life. Supper immediately followed. "Tattoo" was struck at nine o'clock, and " taps" at nine and a half or ten, when the camp must be still, all lights extinguished, and everybody but the sentinels and the officers of the day was expected to be in his bunk. It was more of an expectation, oftentimes, than a reality. I have a distinct remembrance of several occasions, when a few choice spirits had gathered upon the portico of the Adjutant's hut, and, as the story went round, and the wit and fun grew fast and furious, there would come a sudden cessation of speech and mirth — a soothing calm over the joyous turbulence of the hour — as the Colonel's voice would issue from his quarters, "Less noise in camp! Stop that talking!" It was said, (with what truth others may judge,) that the Sergeant Major's voice and the Chaplain's laugh were, at times, somewhat too demonstrative. Once we thought that we had caught the Colonel himself in disobedience to his own orders. A party of ladies and gentlemen had come out from Washington, and after the parade, had remained to spend the evening. They had partaken of the hospitality of our quarters, and the hours of the summer evening wore on with conversation, song and laughter.

The hour of " tattoo " and " taps " had passed, and still the headquarters were noisy with mirth. The next morning, I suggested that it was hardly fair to call us poor subordinates to account, while our commanding officer indulged in unseasonable enjoyment. "Ah! my dear Chaplain," said he, " not so fast. I postponed ' taps ' half an hour, last night." As usual, the Colonel was too much for us.

The duties of the day culminated at dress parade. The brow of the hill was occupied by a large number of spectators from the city, comprising the beauty and fashion of the metropolis. Distinguished men from different parts of the country became our visitors. The President and his family not unfrequently attended. Members of the Cabinet, senators and representatives in Congress, members of the diplomatic corps, men of letters, officers of the army, bishops in the church and dignitaries of state, with many others, both ladies and gentlemen, made our camp a favorite place of resort. Such men as Crittenden, Fremont, Dix, Banks, Andrew, Wilson, the lamented Baker,—even the rebels Breckinridge and Buckner,—have been the recipients of our hospitality and the admiring witnesses of our military evolutions. After the customary exercises of the parade, the regiment was drawn up in close and solid phalanx; heads were uncovered, and the evening service was performed by the Chaplain. A psalm, a brief petition, concluding with the Lord's Prayer, a short sweet strain of music by the band, and the doxology—

"Praise God from whom all blessings flow,"—

constituted our evening offering of gratitude and praise. The service was never omitted in camp, when the parade was formed, and it was the gathering up of the experiences of the day in one fervent utterance of prayer, thanksgiving, supplication and need. In the absence of a description which I myself cannot well give of this scene, I quote the words of one who was more than once an interested spectator:—

"Washington is all one stirring drama; but the 'thing to see,' among the daily sights, is the evening parade and vespers of the Rhode Island Regiment. A lawn of green meadow, lying in the lap of a curved ridge, beyond the grove, forms the parade; and this as the spectator looks down upon it from the terrace above, is the foreground of a landscape in itself absolutely delicious. But the regiment, with its Kossuth hats and glittering arms, and with the quiet tone of its uniforms, completes the picture with wonderful effect. The poetic part of it is prayer. The grounding of arms, the sudden stillness of the drums, the stepping forward of the Chaplain, and the distinct and well-chosen words of the invocation and blessing, left scarce a dry eye among the spectators; and how salutary and elevating must be such influences to the soldiers themselves, needs but little skill for the divining. I can scarcely imagine a righteous battle better prepared for, than by the closing hymn that was sung after the prayer, accompanied with the music of the military band. The voices of the men swelled up like the trained tumult of an advancing host, through an atmosphere that was all aglow with the red and gold of a magnificent sunset, and the smoke of the camp fires among the trees seemed to pause and tremble with the reverberation, the whole scene appearing like a sublime service that had been consecrated by the sudden kindling of earth and sky with an 'unveiling of the Shekinah.' The Rhode Island Regiment should be congratulated, too, I think, on the chance that has given them a leader who looks fully up to it—Col. Burnside's uncovering of his head for the benediction, as he stands before his men, being such a show of intellectual pre-eminence, (phrenologically and physiognomically speaking,) as may well invest it with an authority like that of a sacred altar that is to be borne before them to victory."

One of the most impressive scenes of this kind, as it lies in my recollection, was that of the service performed on the Friday evening before the Battle of Bull Run. We were expecting to march on the following day. At the usual hour, the regiment was formed for parade. Our whole division — 7000 men — were encamped together, a mile or two this side of Centreville, upon both sides of the Warrenton turnpike. Upon a hill, opposite our own parade ground, the Second Rhode Island Regiment was engaged in its evening parade. As its service ended, ours began; and the sweet music of the Second's regimental band, mellowed by the distance, as it floated on the summer evening air, was a fitting prelude to our own service. The 91st Psalm, commencing, " He that dwelleth in the secret place of the Most High shall abide under the shadow of the Almighty," was read. The words of the petition that followed were suggested by the nearness of the day of trial, the voices of the men rose in concert in the Lord's Prayer, and the Doxology was sung with fervor. Men and officers from the different regiments around us gathered about in little groups, to witness the novel scene. General McDowell himself, and his staff, were present, and that generous and gentlemanly officer, when the service was ended, rode up to the chaplain, and, with tearful eyes, giving ample evidence of the depth and sincerity of his emotion, expressed his thanks for the unexpected performance. Then, turning to Col. Burnside, he said, " Colonel, I shall rely upon your brigade." The warrant which he had for such reliance he saw before him. How completely he was justified in cherishing it, the events of the following Sunday fully testified, when that gallant brigade was brought face to face with the foe!

It is not my habit to over-estimate the value of such services. But I cannot help feeling that, upon the souls of those young men, some permanent impression was made. It may have since been overlaid with other and worse things. It may have been enfeebled by the influence of appetites and passions which were held only in partial control. Possibly it may even have been forgotten in some instances. But I am willing to believe that every good thing has an immortal character, and I am safe in saying, that, beneath much of the coarseness and worldliness of the soldier's life, there was and is still, in active existence, the serious and devout feeling which the religious exercises of the camp are calculated to excite. In some hour of lonely meditation, if now it may be dormant, it will be aroused again, and prove itself a blessing to the soul. Many of those men are now on distant shores, and engaged in perilous and difficult duty. They have not forgotten their first campaign. Memory, recalling the past, will paint anew, upon the canvas of the mind, the picture of our evening prayer in our beautiful camp in Washington.

While speaking upon this point I would state that religious services were regularly held in camp, on every Sunday morning. There were but three exceptions. The Catholic portion of the regiment were conducted by the Catholic chaplain to a neighboring church, where they could join their brethren in the form of worship prescribed by their ecclesiastical authorities. The Protestant portion assembled in the grove in front of the headquarters of the regiment. The services consisted of singing, by an excellent choir, organized among the men, under the direction of private Molten, of Co. C; reading the Psalms, with responses; prayer, and a short practical address. The congregation was composed of members of different denominations, whom the pressure of the great principle which they were striving to uphold had united in one common enterprise. Sectarian lines were, for the time, obliterated. We did not ask to what church a man belonged, or what religious creed he professed to believe. We did not meet together for the purpose of discussing controverted topics of religious doctrine, but to help one another in the performance of our duty to our country and our God. While, in furtherance of this view, I welcomed ministers of different churches to the platform which I occupied, I myself was heard with respectful attention by those with whom I differed upon points which did not then come into question. We were all engaged in one great warfare with the world and the flesh, and though we used different weapons, our cause was the same, our spirit was the same, and we all acknowledged allegiance to the same Great Captain of our salvation.

It is well known that a Catholic chaplain, Rev. Thomas Quinn, was associated with me in our regiment, and our intercourse was always of the most cordial and friendly nature. It was another evidence of the obliteration of ecclesiastical lines by the influence of patriotic feeling. I was no less a Protestant. He was no less a Catholic. Yet we could most heartily join hands in this great enterprise of freedom, which we both felt to be thoroughly Christian. The feeling which prevailed is well illustrated by an interview which Father Quinn once had with a chaplain of a New York regiment. After some conversation upon unimportant topics, the chaplain asked Father Quinn, "But how do you, a Catholic, get along with that Unitarian?" "I have yet to learn, Sir," replied my associate, "that religious differences are to be allowed to interrupt that intercourse which is becoming to scholars and gentlemen!"

Besides our usual religious services, there were exercises of the same nature and character in different places in the camp. Under the auspices and inspiration of that true Christian soldier, Lieut. Prescott, a Christian Association was formed, which held meetings once or twice a week, as opportunity was offered, in a little chapel, built for their accommodation. Words of earnest exhortation, prayer, and singing filled the hour, and the meetings were productive of great good. The R. I. Bible Society generously provided us with copies of the New Testament and Psalms. In the quarters of the men and officers, the voice of prayer ushered in the dawn, or breathed its benedictions upon the evening hours. I need not speak of the religious character of our noble and beloved commander. Rarely did he seek his rest at night without engaging in exercises of devotion. "It was his custom at home," he said, in his simple way, and he desired me to continue it with him. In our private conversations, he would speak, with all the trustfulness of a child, of his unwavering conviction that he and all his interests were in the care of a Divine love. Whatever might betide, God's mercy was sure. It seemed to me that a chaplain was scarcely needed in our regiment. For its Colonel's daily life, so pure, so generous, so honorable, so brave, so thoroughly Christian, was more eloquent, in its full-rounded completeness, and more winning and persuasive, than any sermon that I have ever heard from mortal lips. The spirit of his character breathed through the camp, and almost imperceptibly to ourselves, raised every man of us to a loftier plane of life and action. We read in the story of the Psalmist King of Israel, that the love of Jonathan for David "was wonderful, passing the love of women." I knew not the meaning of the passage till I perceived the devotion which Col. Burnside, by the manliness of his life, attracted from every man under his command.

I cannot leave this point without expressing my conviction of the effect and the necessity of religious services in our camps. The very circumstances of the case are productive of influences of the highest moment. In the first experience of a soldier's life, there is unquestionably an incitement of religious feeling. Men have just left their homes, and begin to feel the need of the kindly pressure of home influences. Many of those, who have enlisted in this war, have gone to the scene of danger, impelled by a controlling sense of duty. They feel that there are difficulties in the way; that they will be obliged to endure many hardships; that they may be exposed to many perils, and possibly to painful death. Instinctively they turn to a higher Power, and seek the help of God. Upon such men, religious services produce a wonderful effect. They are a restraint, an encouragement, a direction, a help, and an inspiration. The uncertainty of life, the ignorance of future events, the gradual settling into a state where the prime requisite for success is unquestioning obedience to the orders of other persons, and the consequent loss of self-confidence, seem to induce a strong feeling of dependence upon God. Added to this is the thought, that those who are dear to one's affections must be given up to the care of Providence; and that, for both the distant and near, there are but two things to do,—to wait patiently the progress of events, and to trust in God and one another. The most thoughtless and indifferent man cannot escape the influence of such thoughts and feelings; while those of a deep and tender nature are affected by them to a remarkable degree. As sometimes, on summer mornings, a fresh breeze will set in from some cool quarter of the heavens, and will seem to clear the air of noxious vapors and enervating heat, such delicious coolness and freshness pervade the day; so this fresh gale of duty and patriotism set in upon our wordly life, and, for the time, made it clear and generous and pure.

For the time, I say; for as the heat of summer asserts its presence when the gale is spent, so the old wordliness returns, unless the most vigilant precautions are taken against it. Men, left to themselves, have many idle hours to spend; and the old couplet is true in this as in other cases:—

> " Satan has some mischief still
> For idle hands to do."

Then is felt the force of temptation; then are exercised the influences engendered by the vices of the camp. The body becomes lazy; the mind becomes indolent. The craving for something to excite and interest the attention seeks its gratification in forbidden ways. The appetites and passions are aroused; intemperance, profanity, obscenity, dissoluteness, profligacy, lust, and sloth begin to manifest themselves; and the worst results are threatened. The most dangerous enemy to the soldier is not so much to be found upon the battle-field as in the quiet of the garrison and the camp. It is on the field of the soul that the severest conflicts are waged. It is absolutely necessary, therefore, that all possible religious obligations and sanctions should be enforced; and a chaplain, if he be a truly religious and generous man, can find no more useful scene of labor than among our volunteers.

The sanitary condition of the camp was all that could be desired. Col. Burnside's experience was of the greatest use to his men in this indispensable particular. The grounds were a model of cleanliness, and the quarters of the men were subjected to a rigid inspection, once a week, to insure their neatness. Officers of other regiments, our daily visitors, and the public-spirited gentlemen who were engaged in organizing the United States Sanitary Commission, were unstinted in their expressions of admiration and praise. Our surgeons, Drs. Rivers, Carr, Miller, and Harris, were unwearied in their co-operation with Col. Burnside, for the preservation of the health of the command, and the hospital was as cheerful, attractive, quiet, and comfortable a place as such a building could well be. The strictest hygienic rules were enforced, as were possible under the circumstances, throughout the encampment. The consequence was that there were but few cases of sickness, and before the battle of Bull Run, but two cases of death. Even these could not be traced to any disease which originated in the manner of our life. It is well known that an army suffers more from sickness than from actual conflict on the field of battle. The responsibility of these losses rests with the officers in command. Men in camp are, in many respects, like children, and require constant care. Their life may be made pleasant and healthful as at home, or it may become the source of painful, disgusting, and fatal diseases, almost without number. Not the least of our Colonel's qualifications for command, was his perpetual personal attention to this important branch of the public service.

Washington gradually became one large, extensive camp. The roll of the drums, and the strains of the military bands, seemed to encircle the city with a round of martial music. The streets were filling with soldiers. Scarcely a day passed without the arrival of a regiment from the North. Baltimore was occupied, and the usual route of travel was resumed. Suddenly, and without any publicity of notice, 10,000 men of those who had been coming from day to day, were secretly and at dead of night thrown across Long Bridge, and the ferries, to Alexandria and Arlington Heights.* Then the country was electrified by the death of Ellsworth. Soon, fortifications began to rise, and upon their ramparts bristled the cannon of the Union. The Fire Zouaves, of New York, who once said that "they were sociable with paving stones," had an opportu-

---

* This movement was made on the night of Thursday, May 23. Gov. Sprague left Washington on the morning of this day, and at dress parade, the following Order was read:

CAMP SPRAGUE, May 23d, 1861.

The Colonel commanding takes pleasure in promulgating the following communication from His Excellency, Gov. W. Sprague :

"WASHINGTON, May 23d, 1861.

" I am unwilling to take leave of the First Regiment R. I. D. M. without first bidding, one and all, a reluctant good bye. I have shared with you your anxieties and cares, and would not lose, by absence, the opportunity of sharing with you your first conflict in arms.

" The public service, both State and National, demands my presence in Rhode Island. That performed, accompanied by more of Rhode Island's sons, I shall rejoin you. Bearing the relation of brothers, comrades, we look for approval to our own convictions of an honest discharge of every duty, and to the approbation of our fellow men ; and striving for that, we shall never fail.   **WILLIAM SPRAGUE.**

" To COL. A. E. BURNSIDE,
    Commanding First Regiment R. I. D. M."

nity of improving their acquaintance to some useful purpose. The Seventh Regiment N. Y. S. M. gave ample proof that no gentleman's hands were too soft and dainty to handle the spade and barrow, when his country called for hard work. The Twelfth New York—a popular and gallant corps—was in no wise behind its neighbors, in patriotic duty. The Sixty-ninth made an exhibition of what Father Quinn used to call " the Northern Shovelry," and Fort Corcoran is, to-day, an evidence of its faithful labors. Our regiment, as a body, did not participate in this advance, but it was ordered to hold itself in readiness to support the movement, if necessary. A detail of twenty-six men, under command of Ensign Tower, of Co. E, assisted in establishing, working, and guarding the ferries, by which a portion of the troops crossed the river. Fortunately, the services of the entire regiment were not needed, and the heights that commanded Washington were occupied without opposition. But on the following Saturday, at the very time when the funeral procession of Col. Ellsworth was passing through the city, we thought we were to be called into action. The alarm bells in the city were rung, the signal cannon were fired. Washington was in a ferment. Some of our officers who had received permission to go to their homes on furlough, and were at the railroad station when the alarm was given, hastened back to camp.* The regiment was drawn up in line, with blankets swung, canteens and haversacks filled; the prisoners begged to be released from the guard-house, that they might join in the expected fray; and everything was ready for the receipt of orders to move. It was supposed that an engagement was in progress upon the Virginia side of the Potomac. Firing had been heard, volumes of smoke had been seen, and it was thought that the rebels had determined to drive off the invaders, that were polluting the " sacred soil." The people of Washington were exercised by one of their periodical panics. For the alarm was false, and, just as our regiment was breaking into marching column, intelligence was

---

* The officers that returned were Captains Bucklin and Van Slyck, and Lieutenant Viall, and their presence in camp was greeted with acclamations by the men of their companies.

received that rendered any movement unnecessary. Everything was quiet, and the men, disappointed and uneasy at the loss of an opportunity of action, dispersed to their quarters.

IV.

EXPEDITION TOWARDS HARPER'S FERRY.

A FEW weeks later, the order to move really came. Gen. Patterson, with Gen. Cadwallader as second in command, had projected a plan for an attack upon Harper's Ferry, which the rebels, under Gen. Joseph E. Johnston, had been occupying with considerable force. For this purpose, troops had been gradually concentrating at Chambersburg, Pa., and in its neighborhood. Gen. Scott approved the plan, and upon Gen. Patterson's request for reinforcements, Gen. Scott replied by saying that he would send " Col. Burnside's fine Rhode Island Regiment, with its Battery." At the same time, he advised Gen. Patterson to act with prudence and caution, as the enemy " were strongly posted, and not inferior in numbers,"—advice which Gen. Patterson followed, with too extreme exactness, at a later day, as we found to our cost.

On Saturday, June 8th, orders for our departure were received. During the previous week, rumors had prevailed respecting hostile movements on the Upper Potomac, and even of the crossing of the enemy at Edwards' Ferry or at Conrad's Ferry, near the scene of the subsequent disaster at Ball's Bluff. Pickets had been sent out to guard the road to Bladensburg—one company each night—and a vigilant watch was kept. Our men, therefore, had become somewhat prepared for a movement, and when the order really came, it found them eager to go. They were even glad that the time for decisive action was approaching, and, sending the battery* and baggage forward on Sunday under guard, we marched out of camp, early on Monday morning, 1000 strong. We were to go by rail to Chambersburg, by way of Baltimore. In the

---

* Lieut. Leroy L. Janes, of the Second Artillery, U. S. A., was attached to our battery by order from headquarters, and accompanied our march upon this expedition. His genial and soldierly qualities made him a welcome addition to the artillery officers, and he remained with the battery during its whole time of service. He was an efficient officer, and his short stay with us was most agreeable to all parties.

broad sunlight of that magnificent June day, we marched through the streets of the subdued, yet still at heart, rebellious city. How firmly, defiantly, yet forbearingly the men carried themselves! They never marched better, and they never looked more like soldiers. It was the first time that they had gone through the place, and they went with the air of self-reliant and dutiful men. The white havelocks, which our friends at home had provided, the red blankets, and the blue blouses formed a good combination of the national colors; the regimental band played its most patriotic strains, and the men kept martial step to the "music of the Union." But the citizens were sullen and morose, and as the column filed over the pavements, there were many in the crowd that filled the walks, whose mutterings could scarcely be restrained, and who wished us in a hotter place than were even those broiling streets in the heat of that summer noon. What little enthusiasm was manifested as the front of the column passed, died away before the rear came up, and the companies that closed the line of march, heard remarks not very complimentary to our cause, and not very expressive of satisfaction with the purpose of our journey. Revolvers and bayonets are sometimes great pacificators, and whatever might have been thought and said, there was no overt act. But there was no lack of enthusiasm on our road, however quiet Baltimore may have been. Every village beyond poured out its inhabitants to greet us. Their salutations sounded pleasantly to ears that had not heard a cheer given for the Union for many weeks, and it seemed somewhat strange to feel that we were once more in the midst of loyal communities. On, through that day, we sped, and through the following night and a part of the next day, to Chambersburg, and thence to Greencastle, where we found a most delightful camping-ground among the peaceful Quakers of the Cumberland valley.* We

---

* We were accompanied, upon this expedition, as far as Greencastle, by ex-Governor Dyer, of Providence, who rendered timely and efficient service. Gov. Sprague, then in Rhode Island, hearing of our departure from Washington, immediately left home, and joined the regiment while it was at this encampment. Col. John A. Gardner, Aide-de-Camp, accompanied his Excellency. The camp at Greencastle was, named " Camp Duncan," in honor of Alexander Duncan, Esq. of Providence.

bivouacked in a beautiful grove, through which our men had already turned the channel of a full-flowing brook; and the next morning, pitched our tents for a brief sojourn in this charming spot. Now we were fairly "under canvas," and there is no one of us but looks back, with feelings of liveliest gratification, to the time of our encampment on the Southern border of Pennsylvania. The weather was of the deliciously balmy temperature of early June. The days were clear, and the soft light of a young moon shone down at night among the trees that shaded our encampment. The air was fragrant with the fresh clover and the new-mown hay. The wide-spreading wheat-fields were robed in their richest colors. The distant mountains were outlined upon the Western sky, and were transfigured in the glory of each sunset hour. Through all, was breathing the spirit of a loyal, a patriotic, a thrifty, hospitable and generous people.

We remained here but a few days, waiting the massing of the army which was preparing to reduce the stronghold of Harper's Ferry. But that army was not needed for that enterprise. On the night of Friday, June 12th, intelligence was received that Harper's Ferry was evacuated. Gen. Johnston had withdrawn towards Martinsburg and Winchester, either deceived as to our numbers, or deeming it better for him to engage us in the open plains upon the Virginia side of the Potomac, than to meet our attack in the valley. Whatever may have been his motive, he and his army had gone, and on Saturday morning, at six o'clock, we were again upon the road, expecting to occupy the position which the foe had left, or to meet him upon the soil of Northern Virginia. The terminus of that day's march was Williamsport, in the State of Maryland, where was a ford to be guarded, and where Gen. Patterson's army was to cross. We were heartily welcomed by the loyal people of this town, and found a place for an encampment in a grove upon the eastern edge of the village. On Sunday, a large part of the army forded the river, accompanied by four pieces of our artillery, and encamped at Falling Waters. The residue of the regiment was ordered to be in readiness, as soon as a provision-train should arrive, to march towards

Hancock, to reinforce an Indiana regiment, under Col. Lew. Wallace, there threatened by Gen. Johnston's movements. But before daybreak on Monday, Col. Burnside was roused from sleep by an orderly, who had come in from Hagerstown, with orders for our regiment to return at once to Washington. Gov. Sprague, who had joined the regiment at Greencastle, crossed the river for the artillery, and at seven o'clock, we had commenced our march. A gentle shower, during the night, had cleared the air and laid the dust, and the men, refreshed by a good night's rest, and exhilarated by the bracing atmosphere of the early day, stepped gaily off upon a march, which they did not anticipate would be of seventeen or eighteen hours' duration. We passed through Hagerstown, a pleasant, more than semi-loyal place, where we received friendly greeting, and where the people were under the civilizing influence of a young ladies' seminary, in which Gen. Patterson, with excellent taste, for so old a man, had fixed his headquarters; through Funkstown, a village where bad whiskey and secession, with characteristic affinity, predominated through

Boonsboro', a snug little town, which lay peacefully nestling among the green hills of the region, which afforded us a resting place for two hours in the afternoon, and where our artillery joined our little force.* At sunset, we crossed the South Mountains, through a notch which reminded those of us who had travelled in New England, of the pleasantest portion of the White Mountain scenery, and those who had been abroad, of the beauties of a Swiss landscape. Cascades were falling among the rocks, covered with greenest moss; the foliage of the trees was of the deepest hue, as it hung gracefully over our path; the simple inhabitants of the mountain region gathered to witness the unaccustomed pageant; the golden light of a gorgeous sunset gleamed and glittered along the arms of the soldiers, and flickered among the leaves and branches overhead; the purple haze of twilight mellowed all the scene; music added its charms, and as the column crossed the summit and descended the winding road into the

---

* Gov. Sprague left the battery at Hagerstown, to return home.

valley, the picture was of exquisite and indescribable beauty! But six or seven hours' march was still before us, and we could not linger. We pressed on through Middletown, which turned out its population to greet us, crossed another ridge beneath the broad moonlight, struggled painfully along, foot-sore, languid, and weary, and at last, at half-past twelve o'clock, on the morning of Tuesday, June 18th, we lighted our camp-fires, and sank to sleep upon the ground, on the slope of a hill in the suburbs of Frederick City. We had marched thirty-three miles since the morning, the artillery five miles further still, and yet in half an hour from the time the head of the column arrived at the campground, every straggler had found his proper place in his company bivouac. The rearguard, Co. B, had done its duty faithfully on that day. The next morning, we entered Frederick City, were very hospitably received and entertained by Gov. Hicks and his friends, remained there throughout the day, and, late in the afternoon, started by rail for Washington, by way of the Relay House. We picked up one or two Providence friends on the way, and reaching Washington at a seasonable hour the next morning, were soon in our old quarters at Camp Sprague.

We had an opportunity of noticing, in this journey, the difference of sentiment among the people of Maryland, as it exhibited itself here and in the county through which we passed on our first march; now, and six weeks previously. While, in our first experience, we had occasion to observe the almost utter want of sympathy, and the all-pervading presence of a spirit of opposition to our cause, in the last, we were received with every demonstration of enthusiasm. The inhabitants along the line of our first march, had been told that we were Vandals and marauders, and had removed their property and themselves two or three miles away on either side of the road. The inhabitants of the section, through which our last road lay, had been most cordial and most generous in their expressions of friendship. In the first case, the rebellious, in the last case, the loyal element predominated. The uprising in the North had had, in this quarter, the expected effect. The people of Maryland, either wiser than their Virginia

6*

neighbors, or more easily subdued, had seen that their interest was better subserved in the Union than out of it. Many, without doubt, were at heart sincerely loyal. A large majority did not wish that their State should be made the battle-ground, and they sagaciously determined, in this contest, to cast in their lot with the North. It is true, that a few rampant secessionists were found upon our line of march, and it was thought necessary by some of our men that the emblems of disloyalty should be taken from them. Not only the flag, but, in one instance, the flagstaff was taken ; and I recollect seeing, about midnight, half a dozen men carrying along upon their shoulders, tired as they were, what might pass for a respectably sized spar, upon which the detestable bunting had been raised. They were resolved that that staff should no longer bear a rebel flag. What became of it afterwards, I do not know, but I do not think they brought it home as a trophy. We also found, in Frederick, some rebellious citizens, both male and female. The disloyal Legislature was then and there in session, and a secession paper, which has since been suppressed, was especially bitter upon our regiment and its adventures——after our departure. But we found that the loyal citizens were brave and determined, and the regiment never fared better, during its absence from home, than at their hands.

V

CAMP LIFE RESUMED.

THE remainder of the month of June passed without any incident worthy of comment, except the arrival of the Second Regiment and its Battery. We were glad to greet our brothers-in-arms, who were, in less than a month from their arrival, to prove their gallantry and courage upon the bloody plains.of Manassas. They reached our camp in the gray of the morning, on Saturday, June 22d, and received a soldier's welcome and a soldier's cheer.* Their tents were pitched in our immediate vicinity, and we heartily enjoyed their companionship during our brief sojourn together.

On the 18th of July, our battery left us to

---

* The Second Regiment was accompanied by Gen. Robbins, Secretary Bartlett, Bishop Clark, Hon. J. C. Knight, and other gentlemen of Rhode Island.

rejoin Gen. Patterson's army at Hagerstown, which seemed at last disposed for active operations. I need not say how grievously that officer disappointed us and the country. During our temporary connection with his command, we had known something of his vacillation and unskillfulness. After our departure, he had harassed his troops by marches and counter-marches, and finally, when set to watch his more able enemy, Johnston, he allowed that General to slip off unmolested, to help in our defeat at Bull Run, while he himself was resting in inglorious ease. Our battery saw but little service with the old General, except the drudgery of picket duty. But what our men were there able to do, they did manfully, bravely, and like themselves.

After their departure, we fell into our usual routine of camp life. The Fourth of July was celebrated by our two regiments with oration, poem, and the usual performances pertaining to Independence day. This celebration was conducted with considerable spirit. In the morning, the two regiments, now under command of Col. Burnside as senior officer, were reviewed by the Governor, who, with Col.

Goddard, had come to Washington with the Second Regiment. Immediately afterwards, the two regiments assembled in the grove in which the camp of the Second Regiment—"Camp Clark"—had been pitched. Major Sullivan Ballou was President of the day. Prayer was offered by Rev. Mr. Jameson, Chaplain of the Second Regiment; the Declaration of Independence was read by the Chaplain of the First Regiment; a stirring and eloquent address was delivered by Rev. Father Quinn; and a spicy, witty, and patriotic poem read by Capt. Cyrus G. Dyer. In the afternoon, "Professor Sweet," a private in the Second Regiment, delighted a numerous assembly of spectators with his famous, brain-bewildering "Callacoes" and "Pancraticals." National salutes were fired at sunrise, noon, and sunset. The day passed very pleasantly and peacefully, and without accident of any kind. A week after this, however, the camp was startled by intelligence of a most distressing character. While the battery belonging to the Second Regiment was engaged in drill, on the morning of July 9th, one of the ammunition wagons exploded, instantly killing private Bourn, mortally wounding corporal Nathan T. Morse, Jr., and injuring several other men. Young Morse lingered insensible for an hour or two, and then peacefully breathed his last. Funeral ceremonies were performed at noon by the chaplains of both regiments, which were in attendance, and the bodies of our unfortunate comrades were sent to Providence. This sad event cast a deep shadow of gloom over the camps.

Congress met on the 4th of July. Washington thronged with politicians. The nation became impatient for activity on the part of the army of the Potomac. It seemed as though the time had come for driving back the insolent foe that was menacing the Capital. His presence was regarded almost as a personal insult by the people of the North. Several influential journals, particularly in New York, headed their columns with the motto: "The war-cry of the Nation is, 'On to Richmond;'" and indications of an advance movement began to multiply. Almost every important matter pertaining to the army, found its way into the public journals, and the rebel Generals had, doubtless, full information respecting the plans of the Government. But the plans of the Government, under the pressure of the external influences that were at work, were very hastily matured. Indeed, they were immature. The army was brigaded, July 8th, just eight days before the movement began. Many of the regiments forming the same brigade, and many of the officers commanding them, had not seen each other, or had hardly known of each other. Some of the regiments had been in camp but a few weeks, and were raw troops. The staff-officers were to be appointed, wagon-trains were to be organized, transportation and subsistence-stores to be collected, ammunition and arms to be inspected, trusty guides to be found, reliable maps to be surveyed, projected and drawn, reconnoissances to be made, that the most trustworthy intelligence of the enemy's movements might be gained. But the country, not appreciating the difficulties necessary to the occasion, demanded a forward movement; and a forward movement was made. It was both too early and too late; too early for the perfect discipline of the troops—too late for a surprise. For Gen.

Beauregard was apprised in season to make his dispositions for battle at his leisure, and Gen. Johnston had time to lead the greater part of his army to the assistance of his brother officer.

VI.

BATTLE OF BULL RUN

It was expected that the movement would commence on Monday, July 8th, but it was unavoidably delayed till Tuesday, July 16th. The army consisted of 47 regiments of infantry, 11 batteries of artillery, and 4 companies of cavalry. The infantry averaged about 850 men each, making a force of 39,950; the artillery, 130 men each, 1430; and the cavalry, 70 men each, 280;—the whole force amounting to 41,660 men; in round numbers, 42,000 men, in five divisions.* The

---

* I have probably over-stated this average. The Report of the Sanitary Commission upon the subject makes the average 810 men to a regiment. One regiment had but 640 men on the field. Col. Burnside's brigade—four regiments and one battery—numbered 3700 officers and men. The average of the Sanitary Commission would make the entire force about 40,000 men, of whom at least 10,000 were not within several miles of the battle field.

Seventy-first New York took with it two Dalhgren howitzers. There were, therefore, fifty-five pieces of artillery. Some of the batteries consisted of only four pieces, and one had but three—one 30-pound and two 20-pound Parrott guns. Of this force, fifteen regiments and one battery constituted the reserve, to which were added, on the day of battle, four regiments and three batteries. Of the reserve, seven regiments, under command of Gen. Runyon, forming the Fourth Division, were left in the rear, to follow and hold the line of communication. They did not go more than a mile or two beyond Fairfax Court House. When the army left the neighborhood of Washington, on Tuesday, it consisted of 35,000 men, with the artillery which I have mentioned. This force marched in three columns—one from Alexandria, upon the railroad leading to Manassas, and upon the county road parallel to the railroad, under command of Col. Heintzelman; another, under command of Brig. Gen. Tyler, upon the railroad leading to Leesburg, as far as Vienna, and the road nearly parallel, to Falls Church; the third, or centre column, under Col. Hunter, to which our brigade was attached, from Long Bridge, upon the road leading to the Little River Turnpike, which was the direct road to Fairfax Court House. Col. Miles' division followed Col. Heintzelman's upon the county road, the first day, and afterwards upon the railroad.

Gov. Sprague, with Col. Gardner, accompanied the column as a volunteer, attaching himself to our brigade.* At Annandale we bivouacked; and beneath the clear sky, studded with the sentinel stars, that paced their ceaseless round, we slept the sleep of soldiers, weary with the day's march, indeed, but ready, at the morrow's dawn, to resume our duty. As the different regiments marched into the field selected for the bivouac, and took their assigned places, the scene was very inspiriting. The effect was heightened, an hour or two afterwards, by the music of the different drum-corps, as they struck the tattoo.

---

* Joseph P. Manton, Esq., of Providence, who was visiting the camp immediately prior to the departure of the regiment, accompanied our advance as a volunteer, joining the ranks of the carbineers. In the battle of Bull Run, he did manful and efficient service.

As one ceased, the other took up the strain, and, as the notes rose upon the air, now near, now distant, now full, and now subdued, we almost forgot that we were soldiers, in our admiration of the music. A repetition at sunrise, when the reveille was beat, was ample recompense for our arousal from a sound sleep beneath our blankets.

Our division, consisting of two brigades, respectively under the command of Cols. Burnside and Porter, was on the road at an early hour. Col. Burnside's brigade,* consisting of the Second Rhode Island Regiment,

---

* Col. Burnside was appointed to the command of a brigade, early in July. At the same time, Lieut. Eugene B. Beaumont, of the Fourth Regiment of Cavalry, U. S. A., was detailed as Aide-de-Camp. He immediately joined our regiment, and at once won the high regard of officers and men. A graduate of West Point in the class of 1861, he was a thorough tactitian, and a brave and accomplished man. Modest, unassuming, and gentlemanly, he was yet full of energy and vivacity, and became a most agreeable companion at the table, and a most useful officer in the camp. At the battle of Bull Run, he bore himself with great bravery and self-possession, and deserved the commendation bestowed by his commander, as a "most promising young officer." We separated from him with sincere regret, yet with feelings of unalloyed pleasure, that he had been connected, even for a brief period, with the First Rhode Island Regiment.

with Capt. Reynolds' battery, the First Regiment, the Second New Hampshire, and the Seventy-first New York, was in advance. I mention the regiments as they were formed in brigade, Tuesday afternoon, on Pennsylvania Avenue, for the first time. The order was preserved through the entire march. The Second Regiment, by the express desire of Col. Slocum, led the column. As Col. Burnside was in command of the brigade, and Lieut. Col. Pitman* had been detached for duty at Providence, our own regiment was under the command of Major Balch, and Col. Slocum claimed the front by superiority of rank. Major Balch was most ably assisted by Col. William Goddard, of the Governor's staff, who had been appointed Second Major. We made good progress, though somewhat cautious and slow, as we knew that the enemy's forces occupied Fairfax Court House, and we expected to be compelled to dislodge them. Cavalry scouts and infantry skirmishers were sent for-

---

* Lieut. Col. Pitman left Washington soon after our return from Frederick. Col. Goddard was appointed Second Major of the regiment, June 27th, 1861.

ward, and we gradually felt our way along, passing the smouldering picket fires of the enemy, which had been used the night previous. Suddenly, at a point on the road, about three miles from Fairfax, we found that trees had been felled and were lying across the way. The brush had also been cut away upon the sides of the road, to give a good sweep for the enemy's artillery, in case we should go round the obstruction, instead of through it. We chose the latter, and the sturdy New Hampshire men, with their axes, soon cleared the path. The trees had been felled for the distance of a quarter of a mile, and they were cleared away in less than half an hour. No enemy appeared, and we proceeded once more. Another obstruction was soon found. This time, one large tree had been cut down upon the top of an embankment, and in its fall, it had struck upon its topmost branches, with its trunk in the air. It lay, topsy-turvy, in the road, standing on its head. We simply marched around this. Soon we heard of a fortified camp which commanded our approach. Entrenchments had been thrown up, and a battery of eight cannon was prepared to welcome us. The troops were halted, Col. Burnside rode through the ranks, and in a few well-chosen words, advised the men of the danger in front, and the necessity of coolness and steadiness. Forward again, to climb the hill, upon the summit of which we had seen horsemen, appearing to watch our movements, who rapidly vanished as we approached. We reached the top, and, a few hundred rods in front, stood the earth-work. But there was no enemy. Only our friends of the Second Regiment were in sight before us, with their companies of skirmishers reconnoitering the position. It had been abandoned only an hour or two before. A bank of earth had been thrown up on both sides of the road, embrasures for cannon had been made with sand-bags; and with artillery, properly served, it might have delayed us for a few minutes. But it was clumsily constructed, and could have been carried by one vigorous assault. The officer in command probably found that it was untenable, and his troops were withdrawn. A few articles were found in the grounds, and a mulatto man, who announced himself as the servant of one of the rebel officers, was captured. He had in his possession a sword and sheath, and seemed to have charge of some personal baggage that was lying about the deserted camp. We immediately pushed forward into the town. The color sergeant of the Second Regiment displayed the regimental colors upon the roof of a barn to which he climbed, to attract the notice of Gen. Tyler's Division, whose wagons we saw at a distance, upon the road from Vienna and Falls Church, stopped, as we had been, by fallen trees. The First Regiment marched in to the music of the band playing national airs, and the Second New Hampshire planted the national flag upon the cupola of the Court House. The regiments composing the division were immediately stationed about the town, and Fairfax Court House was ours. Its garrison would also have been ours, if Gen. Tyler had not been delayed, or if he had started an hour or two earlier. More earthworks had been found about the village, and several deserted camps, with a few stands of arms, a mail bag, just arrived from the south, tents, bales of blankets, and medical stores. Our friends had evidently left in great haste, and we certainly preferred their room to their company.

I am sorry to say, that the occupation of Fairfax by our troops was marked, in some instances, by pillage and destruction. Several unoccupied houses were forcibly entered, their furniture injured or smashed to pieces, and many articles stolen and carried away. There was no reason for such wilful destruction of property, and there was no excuse for it. It left enemies behind us, when we might have secured friends. Men, who would have scorned to do such a thing at home, seemed eager and more than ready to lay their hands upon what was not their own. Many things were taken which could not possibly be carried upon the march, and which were thrown aside the next morning, and left upon the road. There was such an element of meanness and of cowardice in all this, that I could not help condemning it then, and I condemn it now. There is some glory in winning a trophy in a fair fight. But the appropriation of private property in a defenceless town, is nothing better than theft. It does not rise even to the dignity of burglary, for that requires a certain amount of courage.

We remained at Fairfax through the afternoon of Wednesday and the following night. Thursday morning, we marched a mile or more beyond the village, and halted in a wood, where we remained through the forenoon, and a part of the afternoon of Thursday. There were rumors of a fight at Centreville. But we could then gain no accurate information respecting it. We remained where we were until our orders came to move forward. We then pushed on, passing a few deserted camps on the way, till we reached a point a mile this side of Centreville, where the whole division bivouacked at sunset, and where we remained till Sunday morning, July 21st. The rebel army was within four or five miles, and the order for battle might be expected at any moment.

Two days were very agreeably spent at this encampment. The weather was delightful, the surroundings were not unpleasant, and though the nearness of danger and duty might have toned down any spirit of undue hilarity, yet we were not without our sources of enjoyment. The song and the joke went round as merrily, and the temper of the camp was as cheerful as at any time in our temporary home in Washington. The days passed peacefully away, and at night the camp-fires of forty regiments lighted up the scene with indescribable beauty. In a day or two, twenty of those regiments were to beat in vain upon the batteries of Manassas, and fall back, broken and defeated. But this we did not anticipate, and we looked hopefully forward to victory; and victory we should have had, if the plans of the commanding General, in the disposition of his forces, had been carried out to their fulfilment.

To explain to the reader the position of the forces engaged, and the battles of Thursday and Sunday, I refer to my diagram. The position of the forces on Thursday, was at Blackburn's and Mitchell's Fords. Gen. Tyler, having spent Wednesday night at or near Germantown, proceeded, early on Thursday morning, to Centreville. He found it abandoned, and, while our division remained on the road as a reserve, he pressed forward to occupy the place. He had understood that

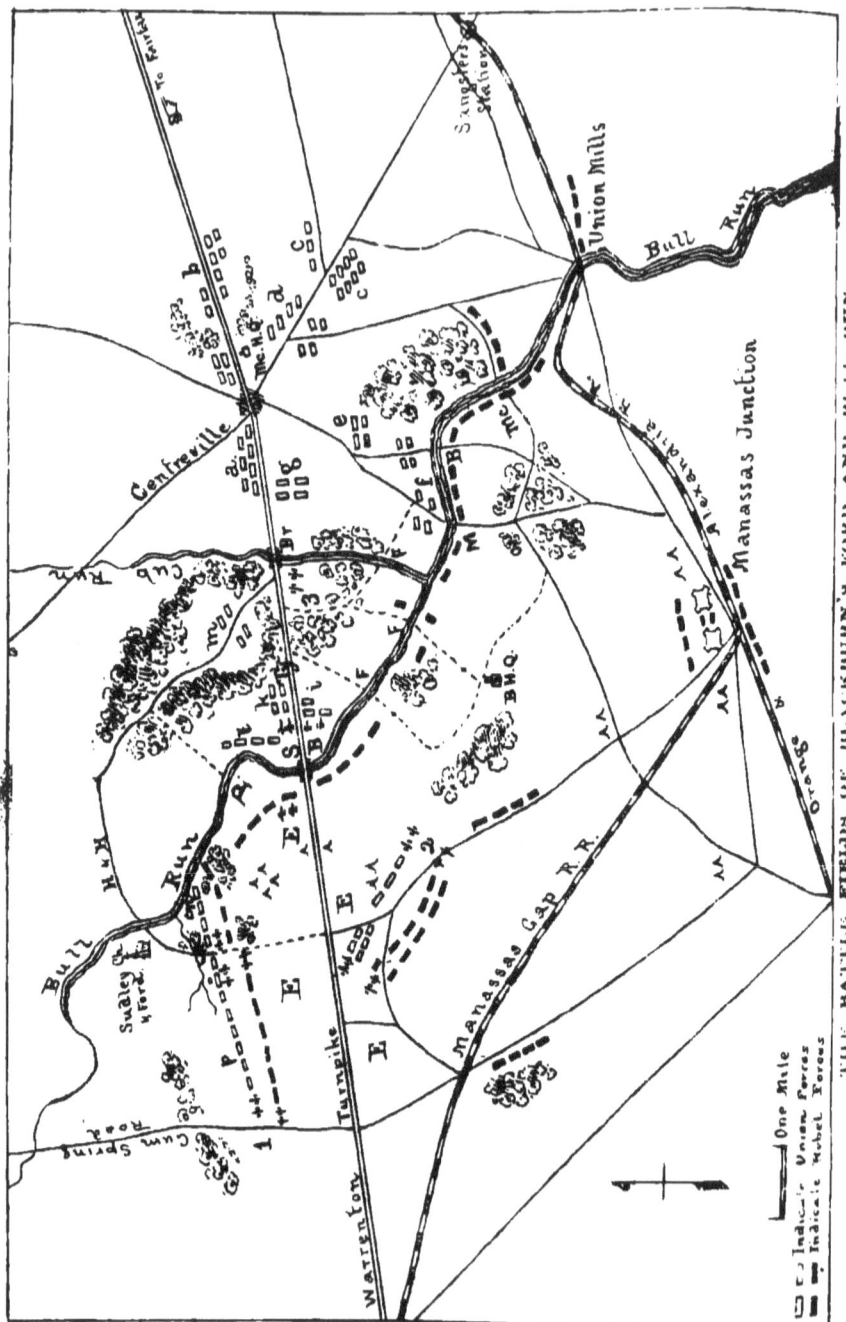

THE BATTLE FIELD OF BLACKBURN'S FORD AND BULL RUN.

EXPLANATION OF THE MAP OF THE BATTLE FIELDS OF BLACKBURN'S FORD AND BULL RUN.

Mc. McLean's Ford. *B.* Blackburn's Ford. *M.* Mitchell's Ford. *S. B.* Stone Bridge. *Br.* Bridge over Cub Run, where artillery was lost. *P.* Poplar or Red Hill Ford, where Heintzelman was to have crossed. *H. & H.* Hunter and Heintzelman's route to Sudley Ford. *Ty.* Tyler's route. *E. E.* Battle field: 1. First position: 2. Second position, where Griffin's and Rickett's batteries were lost. *F. F. F.* Fords across Bull Run and Cub Run. *Mc. H. Q.* McDowell's Headquarters before the battle. *B. H. Q.* Beauregard's Headquarters. ᴀ ᴀ. Enemy's camps. *a.* Tyler's camps before the battle. *b.* Hunter's camps. *R. I.* regiments and battery on the north of turnpike. *c.* Heintzelman's camps. *d.* Miles' camps. *e.* Richardson's brigade, July 18th. *f.* Richardson's and Davies' brigades, July 21st. *g.* Blenker's brigade, afternoon of 21st. *i.* Schenck's brigade through the day, 21st. *k.* Keyes' brigade and *l.* Sherman's brigade, crossed at P. and engaged in the fight, noon of 21st. *m.* Howard's brigade as reserve. *n.* Burnside's brigade. *o.* Porter's brigade. *p.* Heintzelman's division.

the plan of the commanding General was to approach Manassas on the left, by way of Union Mills. With this plan in mind, he detached one of his brigades, under command of Col. Richardson, to reconnoitre the batteries known to be guarding the two fords across Bull Run, between Union Mills and Stone Bridge. A portion of the First Massachusetts, one or two companies of a Michigan regiment, and the whole of the Twelfth New York Regiment, were sent down to the Run. They were fired upon by the enemy's batteries upon the other side, and, after being supported in the reconnoissance for awhile by one or two guns of Ayres' battery, finally retired, having lost a few men in killed and wounded, while the enemy were moving up in great force from Manassas. Gen. Beauregard, whose headquarters were not far from this place, doubtless supposed that we were to make our main attack at this ford upon Thursday. It is my own opinion, that if a general engagement had been brought on at this time, we should have been victorious. Our own men were flushed with the success of the previous day. They had seen the enemy's forces flying before them, and were eager to try their strength. Those forces themselves were more or less demoralized by their hasty retreat. Cols. Heintzelman and Miles were at Sangster's, and on the railroad; Gen. Tyler, with three other brigades, was in the immediate neighborhood. Our own division was resting on the road within call. At all events, whatever might have happened, it could not have been worse than on Sunday. Gen. Johnston had not yet brought down his army from Winchester. Had a quick, decisive blow been struck at that time, it would, doubtless, have been successful. But nothing was done. Richardson encamped his brigade near the position which he had occupied on the field, and the rest of the army went forward and encamped at the points shown upon the map. The result of the battle on Thursday was to check our own advance, and to give encouragement to the enemy. The men had time, on Friday and Saturday, to talk over the matter. Crowds of civilians came out from Washington to view the field, and, in their ramblings, picked up numerous stories and rumors about the bayoneting of the wounded, and the terrible scene of carnage which had been enacted, all of which were retailed with considerable exaggeration. "There had been 1000 killed and wounded"—"Our men had broken and run like sheep"—"The enemy was out-generaling us,"—and other statements, equally extravagant and improbable, found eager listeners. Meanwhile, the army lay motionless; the commanding General had changed his plans, and the ground must be examined anew. And all the time, through the day and the night, the shrieks of the locomotives could be heard by our outposts, as the trains arrived from Richmond and Strasburg, bringing up the needed reinforcements. The two most valuable days of the summer were lost by this fatal inaction.

At last, the movement commenced. We were to start on Saturday, at 6 o'clock P M., but the necessary preparations had not all been made, and the hour of marching was finally fixed upon at two and a half o'clock, Sunday morning. Our division was promptly on the road. The moon was just sinking in the west; a cool wind which had sprung up in the night made the morning chilly; the column proceeded in complete silence, broken only by the quick word of command given by the different officers; the camp-fires burnt with that lurid light peculiarly to be observed in those hours immediately preceding the dawn; the white baggage wagons, relieved by the dark foliage of the forest, had a singularly ghostly appearance, and the ambulances were suggestive of anything but pleasant thoughts. It was Sunday morning, a day not thus accustomed to be observed by those who had been nurtured in New England homes. Altogether, the scene and the time were not calculated to inspire one with any very cheerful anticipations or hopes. Yet the men, notwithstanding their want of sleep, from which the summons to march had roused them, seemed ready and willing to go forward, and we marched through the village with firm, steady, and soldierly bearing. 'Here came a halt. Gen. Tyler's division had not yet been formed. The nearest to the front, it was still unprepared to move. Finally, the column was formed, and we moved forward once more, this time in three parallel lines, one occupying the road, the other two the fields upon either side. We descended the hill sloping to Cub Run. Another halt. Across one narrow bridge which spanned the river, this whole army was to file. Our division was obliged to wait till all of Tyler's division, eleven regiments, with artillery, had passed. When Gen. Tyler had crossed with his command, we followed as speedily as possible. But, of course, our progress was very slow, and when we actually crossed the bridge, men were at work staying and propping the structure, to sustain the weight of our passage. We kept on up the turnpike, as far as the point where a branch road turns to the right among the woods. Gen. Tyler had orders to pass up the turnpike as far as the Stone Bridge, there to make a feint of attacking, till our division, with that of Col. Heintzelman, which immediately followed us, should get into position across Bull Run at the two upper fords.

Gen. Tyler, therefore, went forward, and we diverged from the turnpike to the right. In the fork of the road stands a small building, and near it were Gen. McDowell and his staff, who remained until the entire column had passed on. Emerging soon from the woods, that partially obscured the entrance, we entered upon a large open space, where skirmishers were thrown out by all the regiments, and flanking companies to right and left. The Second Rhode Island led, followed by a wagon filled with shovels, axes, and entrenching tools, guarded by a company of engineers from the Seventy-first; then Capt. Reynolds' battery; then the First Regiment, followed by the Second New Hampshire and the remainder of the Seventy-first, with their howitzers. Col. Porter's brigade was immediately behind us, and Col. Heintzelman's division brought up the rear. From this division, Col. Howard's brigade was retained at the fork of the road, to act as a reserve at this point. The division had also been weakened by the withdrawal of the Fourth Pennsylvania Regiment, belonging to Col. Franklin's brigade, which, with Capt. Varian's battery, from Tyler's division, was, at a later hour, "marching to the rear to the music of the enemy's cannon." The sun had already risen as we passed through this open field, and two distinct reports, coming from the 30-pounder Parrott gun which Tyler had, were borne to our ears upon the morning air. They were not repeated or replied to. The enemy was not yet ready. But we knew that Tyler had reached his position. On, again, through the woods we went, stopped now and then by fallen trunks of trees, which, on this long unused road, had, in some places, accumulated sufficiently to obstruct the way, and occasionally halting for reconnoitering purposes.

Col. Porter, in his report, seems to complain of these delays, and attempts to fasten the responsibility upon " Col. Burnside's brigade." He probably forgot, for a moment, that the division commander, and not Col. Burnside, had the direction of the march, and issued all the orders. It certainly was ungenerous enough for him to make such a return for the labor of Col. Burnside's men, who were clearing the road and examining the woods, that his brigade might pass with ease and safety. Harassed by these delays, the march was somewhat fatiguing, and some of the men became weary for the want of sleep and food. But an occasional nap by the roadside, and a nibble at the hard bread in their haversacks, were all that could be allowed. Forward then we marched, coming out of the woods about four miles from the point where we had turned off. It must have been at this time nearly nine o'clock, and, as we passed out upon the open plateau upon the north side of the Run, we again heard cannonading. It continued briskly for fifteen or twenty minutes, and then ceased. Our friends upon the left were engaging the attention of the enemy, and attempting to divert him from our movement on his flank. But they did not quite succeed. Clouds of dust were seen rising upon our left, from two or three points, betokening the advance of large bodies of men to meet our own advance. We pushed on. Passing through one or two corn-fields, and by a few thrifty looking farm-houses, we at last reached the ford at Sudley's Spring. The day was growing warm. The artillery horses and the men were thirsty, and we passed slowly, allowing our men and animals to drink. At that moment, Gen. McDowell and his staff rode up, with the words, "the enemy is moving heavy columns from Manassas." We again went forward, soon passed Sudley Church, and a moment after, the report of musketry and cannon was heard from the front. Our skirmishers of the Second Regiment had met those of the enemy, and the battle had commenced. Col. Hunter at once ordered the Second Regiment, with its battery, into action. The infantry, with a shout, plunged through the woods which skirted the road upon the left; the battery went up the road, took position with the Second Regiment, immediately upon its left, and commenced firing. Col. Porter again complains that " Col. Burnside's brigade were attacking with too hasty vigor."

It was our brave Second Regiment, sent thus early and unsupported into the fight, not by Col. Burnside, but by Col. Hunter. Then the division commander sent an order to Col. Burnside—not to bring up the balance of his brigade, but—to deploy three regiments into an open field to the right of the wood, and allow Col. Porter to pass us and go upon the field, where our men were contending with fearful odds. But Col. Porter, instead of passing us as was intended, deployed his brigade in our rear, still farther from the scene of action. At that moment, Col. Hunter retired down the road, wounded on the left cheek, and supported by one of his aids. As he passed Col. Burnside, who was in the field, preparing to move his brigade forward, he said: " Burnside, I leave the matter in your hands. Slocum and his regiment went in bravely, and drove the scoundrels." Col. Burnside immediately ordered up the remainder of the brigade to the support of the Second Regiment. The First Regiment, though intended to be held as a reserve, was at once sent upon the field, changing front and charging gallantly through the woods, into which the enemy's shot and shell were falling rapidly. The field beyond was ploughed by cannon balls. This simple statement of facts explains why the Second Regiment was left unsupported for so long a time. It is also to the credit of that gallant regiment, that it thus bore itself so steadily and bravely under the heavy firing of the enemy's attack.'

I am not a military man, and I pronounce my opinion here with considerable diffidence. But it seems to me, that if our skirmishers and leading regiment had fallen back upon the main body, and Col. Hunter had formed his entire division in line of battle, or in columns by divisions, one brigade supporting the other, and then advanced, or awaited an attack, the result would have been different. We should, probably, have overwhelmed the enemy's force at that point, and occupied a position which was almost unassailable, with but little loss of life. The ground was very favorable for such a movement, with open ground in the centre, and woods on either flank. An abandoned railroad track, passing through this field, made a respectable entrenchment. Col. Hunter adopted a different plan, and the regiments went in singly to the battle, marching to the field in one long, straggling column.

The Seventy-first, with its pieces, followed the First Regiment, and took post upon the left of our battery, in the place vacated by the Second Regiment, which had moved farther to the left, to prevent a flank movement of the enemy. Our First Regiment was now upon the right of the Second, and the battle was raging furiously. The Second New Hampshire had gone over to the right, in the field to the rear, and was exposed to a fire which it could not well return. It was immediately ordered up to join its companions in the brigade, and took position to the rear and left of our battery, to afford support in case of case of a charge by the foe. The whole brigade was now upon the field, bravely sustaining the brunt of the enemy's attack. Of Porter's brigade, Griffin's battery, — having driven through the lines of the Seventy-first, — had taken its position, and its supports rapidly came up and took their posts upon his right.

Heintzelman's division had been ordered to cross at the lower ford, but by some mischance had not been able to find the road which led to it. It had, therefore, followed us, and was at this time near Sudley's Ford. As it came up the road, it deployed towards the right, and took position towards the road parallel to that from Sudley's. It is what is called the Gum Spring road, and leads to Leesburg. The position of the forces at this time was as follows: Col. Davies' and Col. Richardson's brigades, (8 regiments of infantry and 3 batteries of artillery, 10 pieces,) at Blackburn's and Mitchell's Fords, and upon the roads, guarding and holding the extreme left; Blenker's brigade, (4 regiments and 1 battery, with Capt. Varian's abandoned pieces, 10 guns.) at Centreville; Howard's brigade, (4 regiments.) at the fork of the Sudley road and Warrenton turnpike; Tyler's division, (11 regiments, 11 pieces of artillery,) at the Stone Bridge, not having yet crossed the Run; Hunter's division, (7 regiments, 18 pieces of artillery,) occupying the field to the west of Bull Run, and upon the extreme right. Heintzelman's division, (5 regiments, 6 pieces of artillery,) was coming up. There were a few companies of cavalry, which were prevented, by the inequalities of the ground, from accomplishing any harm to the enemy. They simply added to the panic which afterwards prevailed. A few days after the battle, the captain of one of these companies, resigning his command, went over to the rebels.

It will be seen, by this statement of the action, that our brigade was bearing the very heaviest part of the battle at this time. At this point, the enemy, passing across the turnpike, in front of Tyler, was concentrating his forces. The roar of cannon, the rattle of musketry, were incessant. The bullets pattered like raindrops, the shot and shell from the rifled cannon, with their peculiar whiz and report, seemed to fill the air. Clouds of smoke hovered over the fray, and shut out the scene. Our men replied most gallantly. The rifled cannon of our battery spoke in thunder. The howitzers of the Seventy-first were bravely and gallantly served. The infantry poured in destructive volleys. Suddenly, in front of the First Regiment, there was a momentary lull. There was a body of men before it bearing the Union flag. "Throw up your muskets, boys," shouted our officers; "for God's sake, don't fire on our own men."

They came nearer and nearer still, then dropping the Union flag and raising the secession banner, they poured in a terrific volley. It was returned with interest, and they precipitately retired before the deadly aim of our cruelly deceived men. We heard from the Second Regiment. Slocum had fallen, pierced with several bullets, our own brave Major once; Ballou had been struck by a cannon ball, which had killed his horse and shattered one of his legs. Tower, once ours, too, like his Colonel, had been shot dead, and others were wounded and killed. We, ourselves, had lost our Prescott so highly esteemed by all, and several soldiers shot and wounded. Our color sergeant had been wounded. One of the guard who had taken the flag had also been struck. Still another, who had taken it from him, had been disabled. Yet the flag was there, waving defiantly in the front and centre of our line. It went into the fight with the regiment, and with the regiment it came out. Thus we were getting on, the enemy pouring up with his troops upon our whole front. Heintzelman was now up, and engaging upon our right, and the enemy was attempting to turn our flank upon the left. The Second Regiment moved farther out and prevented him. Col. Burnside looked over the field. "We must have the regulars," said he, and off he went for them, not thinking that an Aide could induce Col. Porter to send them to our assistance. Back he came with them, charging across the field at a double quick, and with loud cheers. Just then, upon our left, came in sight a large body of men. Who could they be? If the enemy, we were certainly ruined. Anxious eyes watched for the flag. It blew out above the glistening bayonets—the stars and stripes, thank God! It was Sherman's brigade, with the Sixty-ninth New York in front, which Gen. McDowell had sent for, and which, crossing the Run above Stone Bridge, was coming to our support. Steadily forward came the column, and without halting marched round to our position, and formed directly in our rear. Our brigade had been under fire about two hours, more or less.

The enemy had retired, with severe loss, from the woods, which he had obstinately held upon our left and front. Our ammunition was well nigh exhausted. The three regiments upon the left had lost three hundred men, and several horses had been killed in the battery. Gov. Sprague, who had been conspicuous upon the field, assisting Col. Burnside in the disposition of the troops, and Lieut. Weeden, a most brave and active officer in Capt. Reynolds' battery, had each a horse shot under them. But the tide of battle had been turned away from this part of the field, by the steadiness and gallantry of our men. It was time to withdraw the brigade. All the regiments were drawn off into the field in the rear, with the exception of the Second New Hampshire, which still remained, and was afterwards engaged with the enemy in a different part of the field. Col. Marston of this regiment was wounded in the early part of the day. But, with true New Hampshire pluck, he refused to quit the field, and aided by Lieut. Col. Fiske, a gallant officer, still directed the movements of his regiment, which bravely performed every duty which was required of brave men. Capt. Reynolds' battery took a position farther to the front, and did most effective service throughout the action. Leaving Sherman's brigade with Keyes', which had followed Sherman's, and had now come up and was ready to go into the conflict, our own brigade retired in complete order and stacked arms, to receive its ammunition and rest awhile, expecting to resume the battle at a later period. While in this position, the Colonel rode up, and asked: "Well, boys, how have you fared?" Then, as he saw the vacant places, a tear started to his eye. He remembered that he had lost his friend and brave companion in arms, Slocum;

that Ballou, the heroic, devoted servant of duty, had fallen mortally wounded; that his gallant young Ensign, then Captain Tower, was lying dead upon the field; that our own manly, Christian soldier, Prescott, had gone to his reward above the smoke and carnage of the battle; and that many of those whom he regarded almost as his children, had been mangled or killed. He could not keep back the rising tear. It was but for a moment. He brushed it hastily away, and rode once more to the front to meet again the danger. What one of us, who is not absolutely hardened in heart, and bereft of all sympathy with pain and grief, but would esteem him all the more, that he had the feelings of a man as well as the valor of a soldier?

Upon the immediate field where we had been engaged, stood a small one story house. There was a small yard in front, and immediately in front of that, a well of water. The house and yard were full of wounded and dying men, among whom Dr. Harris was hard at work; and many had fallen in the neighborhood of the well. Many others had been brought up from the field. In one room of this house, lay Col. Slocum, speechless, but still conscious and recognizing his friends. It was necessary to remove these persons to the rear. The ambulances were driven up, filled, and returned, again and again. More men were brought in, bandaged as well as could be done at that place, and sent back to the surgeons who were at Sudley Church and a small house upon the left of the road in the rear. Among those who were thus brought in and treated, were Col. Jones of the Fourth Alabama, and several of his privates. Everything possible was done for all, and most of them were sent back. Still, the courage of our men was very noticeable. Not a murmur nor a groan came from their lips. I saw one poor fellow lying on his back in an inner room. "I shall die," said he; "it is useless to do anything for me;" and he said it as calmly and coolly as though sitting in a room at home. He was shot through the spine, and survived for a few days only. While I was engaged at this house, a man came up to me, with a cheerful face and hearty voice. "Doctor," said he, "I am shot through the shoulder, but I do not mean to give it up so. Do what you can for me, and let me go into the fight again." I examined the shoulder, found a piece of flesh as large as an ordinary hen's egg had been shot away, bandaged it for him, and let him go. "Stop a moment. What regiment do you belong to?" "The Sixty-ninth," said he; and back he went into the battle. Not long after this, I walked out to the brow of the hill to see how the fight was going on. Everything was quiet. The enemy had retired far to our right. Upon a distant hill, two regiments were engaged, the federals driving the rebels up the slope. It was either Col. Quimby's Thirteenth New York, or one of the Connecticut regiments. Far off to the south, probably at Blackburn's Ford, I could see an occasional puff of smoke from the enemy's batteries. On the left, at some distance, were a number of civilians and spectators of the battle. I certainly thought the day was won, and I returned to the house, expecting soon to be cheered with the news of complete victory. Everything was promising extremely well. Half an hour later, I noticed that no more ambulances came up, and the field in front was almost entirely deserted. I requested one of the men waiting in the house to go to the rear for an ambulance. He declined doing so. I mounted my horse, which had been quietly grazing, under the fire of the enemy, making up for his lost breakfast, and rode to the rear. As I reached the road, I found it crowded with soldiers, going down the hill. "Where are you going?" I asked. "We are going for water," said they, and pressed on.

I suggested to them that they were going in the wrong direction, and that there was plenty of water in front. But they could not be stopped. I rode to the place where our regiment had halted, stopped a moment, and returned to the road, passing up the hill once more. More soldiers now—the road was full of them, asking, "where is such and such and such a regiment?"—were filling the way. I met Lieut. Col. Wheaton, leading his regiment, the Second, who said to me, "A retreat has been ordered." I was thunderstruck. I had supposed that victory was certain. I knew that the enemy had been most severely crippled, and I had seen his forces on the retreat. The victory had been won, but we had not been able to hold it. The enemy acknowledges himself beaten at half-past three o'clock. But then the fortune of the day took a sudden turn. The enemy's reserves were brought up. They came swarming from Manassas on all the roads. The residue of Johnston's army crossed the fields upon our right from the railroad. Schenck's brigade retired, fearing to be cut off near the Stone Bridge, without having crossed the Run at all. On our right, Howard's brigade, which had just been led forward, was overwhelmed and broken. Griffin had been charged upon, his supports had fled, his men had been shot down, and he had lost all his pieces but one. Rickett's battery had been lost and retaken, and lost again. Wilcox's brigade had been broken, and Wilcox himself had been taken prisoner. Franklin's brigade had suffered scarcely less. Sherman's and Keyes' brigades had pushed on, occupying the turnpike, and south of it, as far as the Gum Spring road; but, seeing the right wing broken, commenced retiring themselves. Our own brigade was rallied by its officers, just across the Run, and remaining till a greater part of the disorganized mass of soldiers had passed, formed in column, and, with the regulars, Arnold's battery, and the cavalry in the rear, prepared to obey the order to retreat. Dr. Harris, who had gone down the hill in front, returned to the church and remained there, sending back a man with a white handkerchief for a flag of truce, to surrender the wounded men whom we had been compelled to abandon. That was the only flag of truce sent to the enemy from our wing, and that was an act of humanity

We retired slowly along the road, up which we had marched in the morning. There was no disorder now. The greater part of the army had gone ahead, and we proceeded at a leisurely rate through the woods. Some one now ordered the artillery and cavalry to the front. They forced a passage through the column. Our rear was only held by the battalion of regulars. We had reached the point where the woods ended, and were coming out into the open space of which I have before spoken, when cannonading was heard directly before us. Just previous, a charge of secession cavalry and a body of infantry had been broken. The truth flashed upon us. Warrenton turnpike was in possession of the enemy, who had pursued Schenck's retreating troops, and it was upon that road that the panic took place, which is so extravagantly described by the letter writers. If the enemy had chosen to bring his battery to the corner of the road, and had pursued our own column, no power on earth could have saved us. But keeping his battery upon a hill beyond, he filled the woods, the open space, the road with his shot and shell. The bridge across Cub Run was soon obstructed. I rode out upon the road and looked around for a moment. Baggage wagons, ambulances, caissons, lay jumbled in strange confusion, while on either side lay the cannon which we had been using. There was the 30-pounder, whose loud report had ushered in the day of battle. There were the howitzers of the Seventy-first, and there four of our own Rhode Island guns, which had been brought safely to this point.* It was a sorry

---

* Two of Capt. Reynolds' guns, becoming disabled, were sent to the rear an hour or two before our retreat commenced. On the road, the guard was attacked by a body of rebel cavalry. One of the pieces, being slung under the gun carriage,

sight; and, seeing the road obstructed, and the enemy's shot falling thickly around our troops, who were here thrown into disorder, I forded the stream above the bridge, and went up the hill on the Centreville side, soon passing beyond the range of the enemy's artillery Upon the crest of the hill, standing at ease, was Blenker's brigade. The Rhode Island regiments rallied at Centreville, and, with the residue of the brigade, went into the camps which they had left in the morning.

The brigades at Blackburn's and Mitchell's Fords were drawn in, and in an hour or two, the whole army was in full retreat towards Washington. We left our camp about 11 o'clock. It was a weary, painful night. The road seemed to stretch on and on. Our men were lame, foot-sore, tired, some wounded, and all more or less exhausted. Still we

---

was abandoned, but the guard succeeded in getting the other across the bridge, and it was carried safely to camp. The remainder of the battery did not reach the bridge till after it had been obstructed, and was there left, the men saving themselves and horses, and the guns, in comparatively good condition, falling into the hands of the rebels. The gun that was saved was afterwards forwarded to Rhode Island, and presented to Gov. Sprague by a vote of the General Assembly.

pressed on, and soon after the dawn, which broke cloudy, rainy, and uncomfortable, the waters of the Potomac and the city of Washington appeared. A few miles farther on, and the brigade collected its shattered forces, crossed Long Bridge, entered Washington in the order in which we had left it on the previous Tuesday, and sought its former camps.

It is a great deal easier for the defeated party to criticize a battle, and show how it could have been won, after the fight is over, than to win the victory at the time. I hesitate to express an opinion upon the military questions connected with this disastrous conflict. I have, however, read the different accounts by various writers with some care, and have given some attention to the official reports of the Generals. The correspondents of the press have in some instances fallen into error, by attempting to describe a battle which ranged along a line of seven or eight miles, instead of telling the story of that which fell beneath their own observation. Some have gone so far as to describe occurrences which could not possibly have existed except in their own excited imagination.

I do not wish to undervalue the obligations of the public to the press. But the narratives of the battle of Bull Run, as published in the journals of our large cities, contain a considerable amount of fable, and are to be read *cum grano salis.*

But it is the battle itself, to which I now wish to direct the reader's attention. I may be allowed, with others, to make a few remarks upon the subject. I have ventured to declare that the battle should have been fought on Thursday, and that the original plan of attacking the enemy by the way of Union Mills was better than that which was afterwards followed. Gen. McDowell wished to push on beyond Fairfax Court House on Wednesday. Such a movement would unquestionably have been advantageous to our cause. It would have prevented much pillaging. It would have placed us nearer the enemy. It would have invited a general engagement on Thursday, which would have given us Manassas Junction. The commanding General states, that the troops were too much exhausted by the march of Wednesday morning. Such was the report of the division commanders. Perhaps the troops themselves were not consulted. It is certain that they wandered over a large area of territory during the afternoon, and it would seem as though their energies might have been as profitably employed upon the march. On Thursday, we should have met inferior forces, and could have defeated them at all points by a vigorous attack. Beauregard would have lost his prestige, and Johnston's junction with him would have been prevented. I do not feel that I am too sanguine in saying, that Manassas would have been occupied, and Richmond have been almost at our mercy. A Persian poet says, " On the neck of the young man sparkles no gem so gracious as enterprise." Would that our generals had worn that gem in the campaign of the summer of 1861.

The affair of Thursday, July 18th, was intended only for a reconnoissance. It was said at the time, that Gen. Tyler acted on his own responsibility, and that Gen. McDowell was at Sangster's Station. However this may have been, it is certain that the withdrawal of our troops on Thursday had the moral effect of a repulse. Several of our wounded men fell into the hands of the enemy, who was encouraged by what he deemed an easy victory.

The attack on Sunday was well intended. But it was unsuccessful. Several causes combined to produce failure. The first lay at the very inception of the movement. It was an independent advance, without support from any quarter. A column of soldiers was pushed forward into an enemy's country, as though it were as easy an undertaking as a pleasure excursion. Indeed, we hardly felt as though we were going to battle. The country did not completely understand what war really meant. Perhaps some supposed that the gleam of a federal bayonet would be sufficient to frighten a regiment of rebels. Gen. Patterson would not or could not move upon Winchester, and Gen. Butler was quiescent at Fortress Monroe. These failures left the available forces of the rebels in the Shenandoah Valley and around Richmond, at full liberty to join Gen. Beauregard at Manassas Junction. Gen. Patterson, in his defence, plainly informs us of a lack of concert of action, and rests the responsibility upon Gen.

Scott. He informs us, that, as early as the 13th of June, (while our regiment was at Greencastle,) he was told from Headquarters, that Gen. McDowell was to make a demonstration on Manassas Junction, and that his own army must be immediately sent across the Potomac. Accordingly, the army marched to Williamsport, and the larger portion of it crossed the river, as I have already said. But the demonstration upon Manassas Junction was not made. On the contrary, the enemy made a demonstration upon Washington, and Gen. Scott at once telegraphed for our return with the regulars and artillery, as the capital was "pressed." We consequently made the forced march to Frederick. Gen. Patterson was therefore obliged to recall his army, and Gen. Johnston assumed a threatening position opposite Williamsport, Clear Spring, and Hancock. If Gen. Patterson is correct—and there is no reason to doubt his declaration—it will be observed, that an advance upon Manassas was projected to take place a month earlier than it was really made. This was foiled, either by the enemy's superior system of espionage, or by secret treason in our own camps and councils, by which the plans for the movement were disclosed. The enemy threatened our lines in front of Washington, at the very moment when we were preparing to strike upon his flank at Winchester, and thus Patterson was crippled at the outset.

Still, the plan of an attack in the valley of the Shenandoah was not given up. On the 2d of July, Patterson crossed the Potomac once more, and in a small affair with Johnston's advance guard, drove him back upon Winchester. On the 9th of July, a council of war was held. and Col. Stone, commanding a division which had marched up from Washington, " spoke twice and decidedly against an advance, advocating a movement to Charlestown." From that time till the 18th of July, Gen. Patterson was in correspondence by telegraph with Gen. Scott, and on the 17th, was informed that Gen. McDowell had taken Fairfax Court House, and would probably carry Manassas Junction on the next day. Gen. Patterson did not wish to take the responsibility of attacking, and telegraphed for instructions. None came; and Gen. Patterson supposed, that Manassas had been taken, and that no more work was expected of his army. There are times when a commanding officer must take responsibilities; and this was one. If he did not choose to attack, he at least could have occupied Leesburg, and formed a junction with Gen. McDowell at Centreville, or beyond. But the golden opportunity passed, and on the 20th, Johnston, to Patterson's knowledge, and without Patterson's interference, marched to Strasburg.

The second cause of the failure of the federal army is to be found in the smallness of the numbers sent to do the work. We felt confident, before we left Washington, that Gen. Scott would not venture to send out an army that was likely to suffer a bad reverse. Had the attack been made on Thursday or Friday, the number was sufficient; but not for the attack on Sunday. Gen. McDowell states that 18,000 men crossed the Run, and were actually engaged. Nineteen regiments and the battalion of regular infantry, were in the principal battle. Four regiments —Col. Howard's brigade—came up near the close, but were immediately obliged to retire. Twenty-four pieces of artillery and one or two companies of cavalry, succeeded in reaching the west side of Bull Run. Fifteen regiments and thirty-one pieces of artillery did not cross the stream at all. Gen. Beauregard says, in his official report, that he had in his possession prisoners from forty-seven regiments of volunteers, and wishes to give the impression that these were full regiments. Besides these, he says, that there were detachments from "nine different regiments of regular troops." "To serve the future historian of the war," he makes these declarations; and, as if to show how much he could impose upon the intelligence of the civilized world, he boldly utters the following audacious falsehood: " Making all allowances for mistakes, we are warranted in saying that the federal army consisted of fifty-nine regiments of volunteers, eight companies of regular infantry, four of marines, nine of regular cavalry, and twelve batteries, one hundred and nineteen guns." He graciously allows an average of eight hundred men to a regiment. " To serve the future historian of the war," I append the statement of the federal force, according to the order of July 8th,* and I had the means of knowing that no additional forces were sent forward, unless there might have been a battery of artillery. Major Barry, chief of artillery, however, declares that there were but forty-nine pieces of artillery in all, as Capt. Varian's battery of six pieces was thrown out of the action, because of the expiration of its term of service. I am not aware of the existence of any data, orders, or documents, which would authorize the General of the rebel forces to make the statements which he does. He over-estimates the number of his assailants. The regular troops, of all arms, were composed of detached companies of different regiments, and we can only explain the mistakes of Gen. Beauregard, either by allowing that he counted each company as a regiment, or by declaring that he has wilfully misstated the case. The federal forces actually in the battle, could not possibly have numbered over 22,000 men. The reserve force, a part of which did not fire a gun, amounted to 13,000 men.

---

* See Appendix.

As regards the numbers opposed to us, we can only make approximations to the facts. Gen. Beauregard admits that he had, of all arms, in the army of the Potomac, 21,883 men and 29 guns; in the army of the Shenandoah, (Gen. Johnston's,) 8,334 and 20 guns; Hill's Virginia Regiment, arriving from the south on the morning of July 21st, 550 men; Hampton's Legion, also arriving that morning, 600 strong; and Gen. Holmes' brigade from Fredericksburg, 1265 men, 6 guns, and a company of cavalry. The total is the very respectable number of 32,632, and 55 pieces of artillery. I think that we may safely conclude that the rebel army engaged amounted to 32,000 men, at the very lowest estimate. From reliable sources, I have been informed, that there were lists of wounded rebels at Richmond, after the battle, belonging to at least forty-two regiments. A writer in a southern journal, before the battle, states that there were from 30,000 to 50,000 men at Manassas Junction, before Gen. Johnston reinforced Gen. Beauregard. Col. Jones of Alabama, who fell into our hands, stated to the surgeon who was dressing his wounds, that the enemy's force amounted to 80,000 men. On the copy of a rebel map, found at Shipping Point, the positions of sixty-three regiments are laid down. The probable truth lies between the lowest and the highest estimate. The enemy was in superior force, and Gen. Beauregard had perfected his arrangements for attacking our army at Centreville, on the morning of July 21st. To his surprise, he found that Gen. McDowell was on the march; and, judging from the affair of Thursday, that the federal forces would attack from the upper fords, he made all his dispositions to meet us as we crossed at Sudley's. While, therefore, our forces were toiling through the unused forest paths, the enemy's forces were rapidly and easily concentrating for our reception. They had the advantage of position, knowledge of the ground, and an abundance of opportunity, by means of the numerous roads from Manassas, of bringing up every available man. Our men were fatigued by a long night march, and had had no means upon the way, of obtaining a proper amount of food. Their haversacks had indeed been supplied; but they were expecting soon to halt for breakfast, and neglected to satisfy their hunger till it was too late. It was certainly creditable to them that they fought so well as they did, and stood so long before retreating. The attack of the enemy amounted almost to a surprise, for none of our Generals believed that he was in any force at Sudley's Ford. The engagement was brought on by the " too hasty vigor" of Col. Hunter in throwing his leading regiment upon the enemy's lines.

A third cause of the federal failure is to be found in the loss of the two most important days of the week, following upon the skirmish of Thursday. It is not necessary here to dwell upon the magnitude of that loss, as I have already stated my reasons for believing, that a greater amount of skill and energy on Thursday would have changed the fortune of the expedition.* Added to that loss, was the

---

* Since the foregoing was written, and while these pages were preparing for the press, the New York Evening Post published what purported to be the report of a conversation between a rebel prisoner of rank and one of the correspondents of that paper. From this report I make the following extract:
" Q. ' What errors do your officers think we committed at the battle of Manassas, that caused us to lose the day ?'

delay of marching on Sunday morning. Gen. McDowell wished to make an advance of a few miles on Saturday evening, and resume the march in the morning. But he was overruled. Col. Hunter's division was ready at the hour, and promptly started. But it had made a march of two miles and more, through the village of Centreville, before Gen. Tyler's division, which by that time should have been across Cub Run, had left its camps. Here was much precious time lost. The formation of Tyler's column was very slow and very

---

" A. 'If you had fought the battle Thursday or Friday, you would have won it. The delay at Blackburn's Ford was fatal to you. You made a great military error in allowing Johnston to reinforce Beauregard. You fought the battle by regiments, while we fought it by brigades and divisions. There were many times, before one o'clock in the afternoon of that day, in which you might have won the battle, if you had vigorously attacked our centre, since the centre of our line of battle had become very weak, by reason of the continual reinforcements Gen. Johnston was obliged to send to the left, which was so fiercely pressed by your right. It was a severely contested battle on your side. Your soldiers fought gallantly, but they were not commanded.'

" Q. 'Why did you not follow up our retreat?'

" A. 'We had no idea of the completeness of our victory at the time; and besides, we were in no condition to follow up the retreat.'"

tedious, and the movements of the other divisions were thus badly hindered. His men had the shortest march to make; they were the nearest to their proposed position. Yet they were the last to be ready. Who was responsible for the delay, it is impossible to tell. But delay there was, and it proved to be fatal. An additional delay was caused by the inability to cross, with any degree of rapidity, the suspension bridge over Cub Run. If it was thought necessary to pass 25,000 men over this stream with celerity, it would seem as though facilities for making that movement should have been provided. A corps of engineers could have been organized at once, the country was exceedingly well timbered, and any required number of bridges might have been built during the two days in which the army was wholly inactive. The engineers did attempt, on Sunday, to build a bridge across Bull Run, near the Stone Bridge, where it was not needed, and where it was not used, except by the enemy to hasten his pursuit. But the suspension bridge over Cub Run was all the facility for crossing the army, and here the most of our cannon were lost, because, upon the retreat, we could not possibly drag them through the stream and up the opposite bank. Here occurs a question, which has not yet been solved. Why could not our artillery have replied to the enemy's guns, that were firing upon us at the bridge? A prompt response on our part might have silenced the few pieces which had been brought to this point. The panic at the bridge must have been of so complete a nature as to prevent the issuing of orders and the working of the guns. When our brigade reached the bridge, everything was lying about in a heap of ruin, and the only duty that remained was that of self-preservation.

Another cause of failure, which, though not chief, was yet, in its effects, accessory to the others, was the inability of Col. Heintzelman to find the road leading to the ford which he had been ordered to cross. Gen. McDowell's plan contemplated a crossing of Bull Run at Sudley's Ford by Col. Hunter, whose division was then to march down the stream, upon its western bank, and "clear away the enemy who may be guarding the lower ford and bridge." Col. Heintzelman was to cross at the lower ford, (Poplar or Red Hill Ford,) "after it had been turned, and then going to the left, take place between the stream and" Hunter's division. But Col. Heintzelman could not find any path from the road up which his division was marching, to the ford, and so followed Col. Hunter. Col. Heintzelman says, in his report, that "no such road was found to exist." It is a curious fact, and one which shows how intelligence is sometimes manufactured for a credulous public, that, at this time, while the third division was quietly marching in our rear, it was telegraphed to a New York journal, that Col. Heintzelman was engaged in cutting a road through the woods, and was within five miles of Manassas Junction. Any one, who examines the map, can readily perceive how great an advantage was lost by this want of success in Col. Heintzelman's search for the forest road. Had his division crossed as was intended, a line of battle could have been formed, of such strength as would have defied an attack. But, unfortunately for us, the two divisions were obliged to cross at the same ford, and the passage was necessarily slow. Unfortunately,

11*

also, a very serious break occurred in our lines, between Sudley's Ford and Stone Bridge, which Cols. Sherman's and Keyes' brigades afterwards filled. When these brigades appeared, and the head of the column with the flag, emerged from the woods upon our left, Col. Burnside and myself happened to be near each other, overlooking the field, and as we saw the approaching column, we both supposed that it was Col. Heintzelman's division, and Col. Burnside mentions the fact in his report. It was a natural mistake, inasmuch as, according to the plan of Gen. McDowell, the third division was to be expected from that quarter.

The necessary extension of our lines upon the right, by the deployment of Col. Heintzelman's division, and the withdrawal of the two fine brigades from Gen. Tyler's division, left our centre greatly weakened. Gen. Schenck's brigade of three regiments and two batteries of artillery, were the only guard to the important position at the Stone Bridge—really the key to the whole line. The enemy saw his advantage, and as soon as possible threw a large body of troops against Gen.

Schenck's three regiments. They had not crossed the Run, and had had no opportunity of participating in the battle. But they had been under a fire which they could not return, during the whole day at intervals, and, as the enemy sent a force across Bull Run at one of the fords below Stone Bridge, to get into Gen. Schenck's rear, that officer thought best to order his brigade to retire. The enemy at once followed, and our troops fell back along the turnpike. The baggage wagons belonging to the army, and the numerous carriages occupied by civilians, were blocking the road, and, as the tidings of the enemy's approach were communicated, a panic took place and the turnpike soon became a scene of terror and destruction. The weakened lines, too long drawn out, gave way on the whole front, and the army of the Union was hopelessly defeated.

Yet there was still one more opportunity. One whole brigade was at Centreville, under command of Col. Blenker. Four regiments of fresh troops, that had been lying inactive, within close hearing of the roar of battle, were awaiting orders to move up. As soon as it was known that the day was lost, the commander of the fifth division, Col. Miles, ordered Col. Blenker to march his brigade to the bridge which crosses Cub Run, and to hold the position at every sacrifice. This was for the purpose of protecting our retreating troops as they emerged from the by-road near the bridge, and to hold the pursuing enemy in check. Artillery was to have been sent with Col. Blenker's brigade. Had this movement been made, there can be no question of its beneficial result. Col. Heintzelman expresses the opinion, that had the brigade been moved up the turnpike, "near one-third of the artillery lost might have been saved." Of the correctness of this opinion, there can be no doubt. Not only would the artillery have been saved, but also the honor and morale of the army. Here was the point where the greatest demoralization took place. Col. Miles, with the eye of an old soldier, saw the importance of the position, and he made the necessary provision for its security. He ordered the only brigade which could be moved to take and hold the place. His order was not obeyed. Col. Blenker marched his brigade through the village of Centreville to the heights overlooking the bridge, which were entirely beyond the range of the enemy's artillery, but went no farther. Col. Blenker says, that the road was full of fugitives. But the fields were open to him on either side; and had his troops been moved to the position as intended by Col. Miles, an hour or two earlier in the day, our retreat would have been effectually covered. The enemy's batteries would have been silenced. A stand at Centreville could have been made, till reinforcements had reached us from Washington, and the disaster which we had suffered would have been retrieved.

The disposition of the reserves upon the day of battle, is a point which has given rise to considerable discussion. Cols. Richardson's and Davies' brigades could not be moved, as they were imperatively needed at Blackburn's and Mitchell's Fords, to protect our rear. They were admirably posted, and though not actively engaged, did excellent service. But the enemy was in force in front, and they could only make demonstrations in order to prevent reinforcements from that point to the enemy's left. Col. Miles and Richardson both wished in the morning to storm the batteries of the enemy upon the other side of Bull Run. But, upon examining their instructions, they found themselves positively forbidden to do more than to hold the position. A successful charge at that point at 12 or 1 o'clock, might have given us the victory, along the whole line. But it could not have been made without transcending the order of the commanding General, and Col. Miles thought himself not authorized to do that. It was part of Gen. Beauregard's plan to attack our own lines from Union Mills, and an order to that effect was sent to Gen. Ewell, commanding the extreme right of the enemy's army. But the order never reached that officer, and both our own forces and the rebels stood facing each other through the day, without an advance movement of any importance upon either side. The enemy threw one brigade across Bull Run, to threaten the road to Centreville. in the morning, and again at noon, both of which attempts were gallantly met and the enemy's force repulsed by Col. Davies. The brigade of Gen. Ewell was marched from Union Mills to Stone Bridge, and Gen. Jackson's brigade reinforced the enemy's left by marching from Mitchell's Ford. Our own brigades made no movements except as demonstrations. Later in the day, when they were withdrawn from the Run to the heights of Centreville, a quarrel arose between Cols. Miles and Richardson, in regard to the disposition of one of the regiments of Col. Richardson's brigade. Col. Miles was accused of drunkenness, and Gen. McDowell, arriving at Centreville at the time, solved the difficulty by taking the fifth division under his direct command. Col. Richardson had been attached to Gen. Tyler's division prior to this time, but was assigned to the reserve on the day of battle. Col. Richardson was impulsive and excited. Col. Miles was indignant and irritated by the insubordination of his inferior officer, and by the confusion that everywhere prevailed. His own orders were not obeyed, and the disposition of his forces was changed by other officers for the worse. It is easy to make a charge of intoxication under such circumstances. But the Court of Inquiry that was afterwards convened to try the case, found that the evidence adduced was not sufficient to substantiate the charge. I have no desire to excuse incompetence or misconduct on the part of any person. But Col. Miles, as acknowledged even by his prosecutors, made very judicious arrangements for covering the retreat of our troops.

The chief objection to the disposition of the reserve, appears to consist in the distance at which it was placed on the day of battle. Gen. Runyon's division, which was properly the reserve, was not within seven miles of Centreville, till after the day was lost. Three regiments were then brought up to aid in checking the enemy's pursuit. What Gen. Runyon's division might have done, had it been brought to the vicinity of Centreville on Saturday, and allowed Col. Miles' division to have crossed Bull Run at Blackburn's Ford on Sunday, to attack the enemy's right and centre, is, of course, only a matter of conjecture. The simple fact remains, that the actual reserve of the army of the Potomac, on Sunday, July 21st, was not within supporting distance, and could not be brought into the field. While the enemy was bringing to his endangered lines all available forces from every quarter, we made no effort whatever to draw reinforcements from Washington, or even to engage the services of our own special reserve. Gen. McDowell says: Gen. Runyon's "advanced regiment was about seven miles in the rear of Centreville," or about twelve miles from Stone Bridge, and fourteen or fifteen miles from the battle field.

Yet, notwithstanding all these disadvantages, it is clear, that the army of the Union was uniformly successful up to three o'clock in the afternoon—having manfully performed a most fatiguing march, and fought a severe and, till that time, a winning battle. Thirteen hours' service was a good day's work. One hour more of steady bearing would have crowned our arms with victory. But the commanding General and the troops were not quite equal to the occasion, and the order was given to retreat. The retreat became a rout, and the rout a panic.

One great cause lay back of all the rest: the deficiency of discipline on the part of officers and men. How hard it is for men to learn the lesson of obedience! Near the field, and even on the field, where personal safety positively required that every man should be in his place, there were stragglers. Men left the ranks by twos and threes. Captains lost their companies, and companies their captains. Unauthorized persons gave confused and contradictory orders. Regiments almost imperceptibly became disorganized and melted away. The commanding General himself was hardly master of the situation. No army in the world could have stood under circumstances like these; and when the final advance of the enemy was made, there was nothing left to the regiments that still remained unbroken, but to retreat in as good order as possible. It was done, with the conviction on the part of many, afterwards confirmed, that the enemy was in as bad a plight as themselves. Men cannot be brave who are undisciplined in virtue. Even brave men must learn how to direct their energy and courage aright, to accomplish the most effective results. Not superiority of arms and equipments, but enterprise, spirit, an indomitable will, an obstinate persistence, directed, disciplined and trained, assure the victory. Skill and drill are the magic watchwords of success.

But suppose that a victory had been gained on the plains of Manassas by the federal forces. What would have been its results? I doubt if the nation would have been in as good condition at this day, as it really is in consequence of the defeat. Our forces might have occupied Manassas, and even gone to Richmond. I fear that success at that time would have caused a diminution of earnestness. We should have deemed the conflict easy. We should have considered our task as of slight importance. We should have become careless, self-confident, and too credulous of the future, and, by our easy-going, heedless trustfulness in ourselves and our cause, have laid ourselves open to a more disastrous defeat at a subsequent day. We needed a defeat to concentrate the energies of the nation; to convince the people of the importance of the struggle; to teach them that Providence had given them the mightiest work to which a people could be called, and in whose issues, the welfare of the human race was involved. It is no light matter, which is to be determined by a single summer day's conflict, to fight the battles of freedom and civilization for a continent and an age.

Perhaps the most dangerous result of victory would have been, to call into existence and powerful activity a party determined upon peace at any price. The North would have been told: "You have been victorious in a pitched battle, upon the open field and against superior numbers. You have humbled the pride of the South. Be magnanimous now, and grant the South what she wishes." We should have heard of "compromise" once more. The struggle, prematurely ended, would have resulted in an increase of influence, and in the virtual victory of the principle of secession. We needed a defeat to assure us that we were really at war—at war with a desperate and determined foe; and that we could not have a genuine peace till we had overcome, in severe conflicts, the power which, beneath the surface, had long been and would continue to be, unless it be subdued, at utter enmity with all that is great and good in American life. The nation has learned at Manassas, that it is civilization and barbarism, freedom and slavery, republicanism and despotism, engaged in a life and death grapple—fighting for the possession of a continent. The nation has learned that THE UNION stands for all that is best and noblest in the civilization of the nineteenth century —" the best government that the world ever saw." When it has been fairly established, beyond the reach of domestic treason, and above the malice, jealousy, and enmity of foreign foes, we shall value it all the more for what it shall have cost, of treasure, blood, brave men's lives, and loving women's desolated hearts. The Republic will stand forever firm. Intestine strife will never again tear its vitals. The nations of the world will admire and esteem a people whose magnificent energies have been engaged in the service of the highest welfare of man—a people that has been willing to spend all, to suffer all, and sacrifice all for the sake of self-government, liberty, and impartial justice!

VII.

CONCLUSION

What took place after the battle of Bull Run, requires but little comment. Col. Burnside had his orders on Wednesday to return with his regiment to Rhode Island, but declined complying with them till he had ascertained from Gen. Scott, that there was no immediate prospect of an attack by the rebels upon Washington. Had there been any such expectation, the regiment would certainly have remained to share in the defence. But Gen. Scott assured our commander that there could be no attack, and the prediction of the veteran has been verified. It was therefore thought best that the regiment should return home, with the hope that most of its members would re-enlist.*

---

* See Appendix D.

We left Washington at midnight, on Thursday, and partook most gratefully of the hospitalities of the citizens of Philadelphia on the way. On Sunday, July 28th, the regiment reached Providence. Proceeding by transports from New York, we arrived below the city at daylight. Hearing that extensive arrangements had been made to receive the returning troops, Col. Burnside ordered the steamers up the harbor. The regiment disembarked at six o'clock. Again, the streets of Providence were crowded. The chartered companies of Providence, Pawtucket, Newport and Woonsocket performed escort duty, and the grateful procession moved through the principal avenues of the city, greeted with joyful cheers and acclamations by the multitudes that had gathered to welcome our return. Public services were omitted in the churches for the morning, as all felt that the coming of those who had nobly done their duty in scenes of danger, and the expressions of· gratitude which their appearance called forth, were most acceptable worship to the God whose love had been their safeguard. Tears fell from many an eye, as those were remembered whose places in the ranks were vacant, and the gladness that crowned the hour was tempered with the serious recollection of the captives and the dead. As the column thus pursued its march, the officers and soldiers covered with flowers, it was like a moving panorama of beauty, gratitude, and joy. Halting in Exchange Place, the soldiers stacked their arms, and marching into Railroad Hall, were addressed in words of welcome by Hon. Samuel G. Arnold and Bishop Clark. Prayer was offered by the Bishop, a substantial breakfast was partaken, and the different companies were afterwards dismissed to their homes. On Friday, August 2, the regiment was mustered out of the service of the United States, and disbanded. On Wednesday, July 31, the battery of light artillery arrived home, and on Thursday morning the officers and men were welcomed by Hon. Thomas A. Jenckes.[*] They were mustered out a few days later.

The prisoners, with one or two exceptions, have been released, and while the memory of

---

[*] See Appendix E.

the valor of our fallen comrades is our undying possession, the example of their virtue and self-sacrifice shall be to us a perpetual inspiration. When peace shall come again, or Virginia be re-possessed, we will gather up their sacred dust and pay to it the honors due to our heroic dead.*

Nor will we forget the debt of gratitude we owe to the living. To two men the State of

---

* On the 9th of March, 1862, Manassas was evacuated by the rebels. A week or two later, Gov. Sprague, with Mr. J. W Richardson, and another gentleman from Woonsocket, who had witnessed, as prisoners of war, the sad scenes at Sudley Church and vicinity after the retreat of our forces, proceeded to Washington to procure the remains of the officers of the Second Regiment, who had fallen. An escort of cavalry was provided, and the party repaired to the battle field, reaching the place on Friday, March 21st, and remaining there during that day and the following. A day later, another party, consisting of Lieut. L. J. Warner and Messrs. S. G. Trippe and J. Harry Welch, reached the place to search for the remains of Lieut. Prescott. The remains of Col. Slocum, Maj. Ballou, and Capt. Tower were disinterred, and afterwards brought to Providence. On Monday, March 31, public honors were paid by the State authorities to the memory of these gallant men, in which large numbers of the military of the State participated. The body of Lieut. Prescott was not found, and no public demonstration has as yet attested the estimation in which his christian character and bravery of soul are held by his late-comrades in arms.

Rhode Island is under lasting obligations. Their names should be cherished as household words in every Rhode Island home. I am anticipated when I mention the names of AMBROSE E. BURNSIDE and JAMES HARRIS. For courage without rashness, for prudence without fear, for a quick sense of honor which scorned all baseness, for a high-minded generosity which frowned upon all petty jealousy and mean intrigue, for self-devotion to the interests of the State and country which reposed in him their confidence, and for self-sacrifice to this great cause of Liberty and Union, Col. Burnside was and is distinguished more than any man whom I have ever known. He sought from this service no personal glory, no mere military distinction, which has such charms for weaker men. He desired no pomp, no parade, no flattery, no preferment. He simply wished to do his duty to the men under his command; to the parents, sisters, wives and friends who had entrusted these precious lives to his keeping; to the State which had recognized his abilities, and had sent him forth; to the country which needed his counsels and his arm; to God, who has so richly endowed him with every quality that marks a man. How well he did his duty is well known, and history will record. Those were his public characteristics. To myself, who had the privilege of his confidence, his friendship, and his private intercourse, his life was a daily wonder and a daily admiration. Every thought and every act was for the welfare of his regiment. By day and night, his vigilance secured the comfort and the happiness of his command. He marched on foot that he might measure the endurance of his men by his own. He lightened every hardship by sharing it with them. He diminished every danger by his care for their safety In every encampment, his own quarters were the last to be selected and the last to be prepared. His private funds were more than once drawn upon, and his generosity perpetually exercised, that his men should not suffer for the want of any needful thing. It was his regiment first, himself always last. Is it any wonder that we should love him with a surpassing devotion? Let other and greener laurels encircle his brow, and let him wear even a loftier title than that which now he bears with equal modesty and faithfulness. He will be honored by us, to whom he was like a parent in his unselfish love, as our brave, simple-hearted, manly Colonel.

I know that my comrades will not think me invidious in choosing from their number our fearless young surgeon, for especial mention in this place. I know that they will thank me for giving expression to those feelings which stir their own hearts. In the camp and on the field, Dr. Harris was equally assiduous, cool, self-possessed, and efficient. Riding in the front with the Colonel of the Second Regiment, to which he had been temporarily attached, he was among the earliest on the field upon the day of battle and carnage. His professional services were at once called into requisition, and from the beginning to the end—nay, beyond the end of that bloody strife, he never left his post of duty. Always at work and active, he did all that man could do to alleviate the sufferings and soothe the pain of our wounded and dying men. He had a kind word and a gentle touch for all. Forgetful of himself, he only wrought for others. He had indeed a less conspicuous duty than those who fought upon the field. But never was a more necessary duty more faithfully performed. The wounded of the enemy who fell into our hands were as carefully and tenderly treated as our own men. Not content with the labor which he performed upon the summit of the hill, upon which the battle commenced, he went down into the valley and the woods that had been held by the opposing forces, and there still labored till after the retreat commenced. Then, going to the rear, he remained at the hospital at Sudley Church, to do still more for those who were in need. Then, giving himself up a prisoner, he went to Richmond, and would not accept his release till the Rhode Island soldiers were out of danger, or beyond the surgeon's skill; and, after his return, still busied himself here and at Washington for the release of the wounded prisoners who as yet remained in the hands of the enemy. The simple story is his sufficient eulogy, and I need not add a single word more to express the admiration of my comrades and my own for the noble, self-sacrificing and devoted conduct of our valued friend.

The First Rhode Island Regiment no longer exists. Its flag, pierced with bullets, is in the possession of the State, an evidence of the valor of its defenders.* A large proportion of its members have already joined the other regiments that have gone out from us, and are actively employed in the service of their country. God's help and blessing go with them and their fellow soldiers! Wherever they go—those men from these Rhode Island homes—we may rest assured that the honor of our State is in the keeping of brave men; and when this war is ended, and the flag of the Union once more floats peacefully to the breeze, from sea to sea, the names of these Rhode Island troops, infantry, artillery, cavalry and all, will be written in brightest lines upon the pages of our nation's history. Let us who still remain behind, be faithful to them as we know they will be faithful to us.

---

* See Appendix F.

APPENDIX A.

THE THREE MONTHS' VOLUNTEERS.

THE Three Months' Volunteers were called to meet an emergency. They responded with the utmost readiness. In the case of our own regiment—and this is but one out of many—men left their business, their families, their all, at a few hours' notice. Some relinquished important enterprises. Some changed their entire plans of life. Some gave up contemplated visits abroad. Some hurried home from abroad to strike one blow for the country, which was all the dearer to them for its peril, and for their separation from its shores. These volunteers nobly met the emergency which had summoned them. They hurried to Washington. They saved the capital of the nation from destructive foes. They saved the government. A few weeks' delay would have been fatal. The bravery, the skill, the adaptedness to novel circumstances, which they displayed, were the hope of the country, and the assurance of stability in the maintenance of the State. Public attention has been so much centred upon Washington, as sometimes to induce a partial forgetfulness of the great services rendered by these men in other parts of the country. St. Louis and Missouri; Cairo and Southern Illinois; Western Virginia, Annapolis, Baltimore, and the State of Maryland; Fortress Monroe, with its perpetual threat of Norfolk and Richmond, and its command of Chesapeake Bay; Fort Pickens, Key West, the Tortugas, and the Florida Keys, with the command of the Gulf of

Mexico, belong to the country to-day because of the timely assistance and the energetic work of the three months' volunteers. They built Fort Corcoran, Fort Albany, Fort Runyon, and Fort Ellsworth. They first occupied the soil of Virginia. They drove Gen. Johnston out of Harper's Ferry, and occupied and re-possessed that place, which was one of the first that the Government had been obliged to abandon. They could fight, as well as work. They proved their bravery at Grafton, Phillippa, Romney, Booneville, Carthage, Buckhannon, Rich Mountain, and Barboursville, and even the disastrous fields of Big Bethel, Bull Run, and Wilson's Creek were illustrated by their valor. At Bull Run, the courage and endurance of the three months' volunteers were amply proved. Such regiments as the Thirteenth, Sixty-ninth, and Seventy-first New York, Fifth Massachusetts, First Michigan, First and Second Maine, First and Second Connecticut, not to mention others, suffered no disgrace upon that scene of defeat. The term of service of several of these regiments had already expired, as was the case with our own regiment, yet they marched to the battle field with cheerfulness and alacrity. They would have been willing to remain at Washington long afterwards, had the Government so desired. But those who understood the real nature of the case, thought it advisable rather to re-organize the army, than to keep these men in service. It is hardly necessary to notice the sneers and slurs of the English correspondent of the London Times upon the return of the three months' volunteers, and their reception at home. The criticism of the Times and its sympathizers is at once so ignorant and so ill-natured, so full of detraction and a desire to make the worse appear the better reason, as to merit little attention. The first volunteers can point to their record for their vindication. They were received with public rejoicings, because the people of the country were desirous of making grateful acknowledgment of their obligations to those who had saved the Republic.

Moreover, the three months' regiments have been schools of

THE THREE MONTHS' VOLUNTEERS.   149

instruction for many of the officers of the regiments for three years. From statistics which I give in another place,* it will be seen how largely the other regiments from our own State are indebted for their officers to those who had already served in the First Regiment. I presume that this is not a singular case. Other States doubtless show a similar result. Had the service for the short term been productive of no other fruit than this, it would be sufficient to give the early volunteers a high place in the regards of their fellow citizens. The regular service itself is filling up its depleted lists by calling the officers of the three months' regiments to honorable positions in the army.

The moral effect of the uprising of the people, as manifested in the action of the early volunteers, must be taken into the account in making up our judgment. Men engaged in peaceful occupations at once became soldiers. It was proved, that American citizens, of every grade in life, and of every kind of employment, possessed the capacity, the will, and the courage of well-trained armies. A reference to the table of occupations will show how readily our people can take arms into their hands for the defence of their country's institutions. The large army of seventy-five thousand men was simply the advance guard. The loyal States have sent over five hundred thousand men to form the main body, and they have all shown that volunteers can stand, like veterans, beneath the heaviest fire which the most effective engines of destruction can produce. A training of three years, should the war continue, will make of this army an invincible host, which no foreign power will be in haste to meet. But the policy of the American nation is peace with all the world, if it can be secured honorably; and the nations of Europe will see the survivors of the war returning to their usual occupations, and resuming their former life as good citizens, obedient to law and observant of the rules of public order. As it

---

* See Appendix D.

is, so far as numbers are concerned, they are scarcely missed from our Northern communities, and the business of our towns and cities and villages goes on as usual. There are no mobs, there is no destitution, there is no lack of generous assistance to all who in any way may be in want. The soldiers who have gone, and the people who have sent them, are proving themselves worthy of the institutions which they are defending and supporting. God be praised that American manhood, American valor, and American loyalty have exhibited such noble characteristics before the eyes of all mankind.

APPENDIX B.

THE SEA GULL AND HER CARGO.

I HAVE alluded to the generosity of our friends in sending to the Rhode Island soldiers, while in camp, a full cargo of ice. Messrs. Earl Carpenter and Sons, and the Providence Ice Co. united in contributing from their storehouses, a quantity of ice sufficient to load the schooner Sea Gull. Mr. John Kendrick was especially active in procuring subscriptions for the expense of chartering the vessel and for other necessary payments. The Sea Gull was freighted with a large number of packages of different kinds, sent by the friends of the soldiers. She set sail from Providence, May 21st, 1861, and arrived at Washington on the 27th. A large quantity of clams and fish had been put on board, with the hope that Rhode Island in the camp might celebrate "Election Day" (May 28th) with a genuine "clambake." It was intended to issue invitations to the President and the Cabinet to share our festivities. But alas for human expectations! The voyage wrought sad havoc with the most perishable part of the cargo, and the clams found a congenial burial place in the mud at the bottom of the Potomac. The remainder of the cargo was distributed among the men, and was received with the liveliest expressions of satisfaction. "Election Day" had its concomitants of "egg-nog" and "blue eggs" in the quarters of Company F, and a salute of thirty-four guns at sunset celebrated the inauguration of the State Government at Newport.

APPENDIX B.

On the following Sunday, at dress parade, Col. Burnside caused the following order to be read:

June 2d, 1861.

The Col. commanding takes this occasion to express, in behalf of the regiment, his grateful acknowledgments to the donors of a cargo of ice, which has been recently received from Providence, by the schooner Sea Gull, viz.: to

A. & W. Sprague,	Isaac Hartshorn,
A. D. & J. Y. Smith,	Thomas Davis,
E. P. Mason & Co.,	Corliss Steam Engine Co.,
Thomas Hoppin,	Bradford, Miller & Simons,
Alexander Duncan,	Thomas J. Hill,
J. W. Slater,	Cook & Danielson,
J. Carter Brown,	Edward Harris,
R. H. Ives,	H. T. Beckwith,
A. Manton,	I. H. Day,
Day & Chapin,	D. C. Jencks,
W. W. Hoppin,	J. H. Mason & Son,
Orray Taft & Co.,	A. O. Peck,
Thomas A. Jenckes,	John Pitman,
Bradford Taft & Co.,	W B. Snow, Jr.,
A. B. Dike,	S. Sterry Smith,
Knowles & Anthony,	W & S. G. Coleman,
Mrs. Moses B. Ives,	Day & Sprague,
Miss Ives,	Taylor, Simonds & Co.,
Congdon, Aylesworth & Co.,	R. Currey,
H. Lippit & Co.,	Benjamin Dyer,
A. Thayer,	

and six gentlemen whose names are unknown.

Thanks are also due to the indefatigable exertions of John Kendrick, to Earl C. Potter, and the following named gentlemen who accompanied Capt. Howland as guard to the vessel, viz.:

Rev. S. W. Field,	O. W. Frieze,
E. L. Walcott,	J. A. Howland,
D. T. Downe,	H. S. Harris, and
A. E. Bradley,	H. J. Smith, of Providence,
E. S. Allen,	P W. Lippitt, of Woonsocket,
J. A. Winsor,	Wm. Town, of Pawtucket.

The donation of five hundred copies of the New Testament and Psalms, from the R. I. Bible Society, is also thankfully recognized, as is the generosity of that host of friends of the regiment, whose good will towards us has been so abundantly manifested in the numerous gifts with which the Sea Gull was freighted.

APPENDIX C.

THE DEAD.

JOHN S. SLOCUM. This gallant officer, at the time of his death in command of the Second Regiment Rhode Island Volunteers, was born in Richmond, R. I., in the year 1824. Of a decidedly military inclination, he early in life became a member of a volunteer corps of our State militia. When the war with Mexico broke out, he was appointed lieutenant of a company in the famous Ninth Regiment, (Col. Ransom's.) He was in several of the important battles on the route from Vera Cruz to the city of Mexico, and distinguished himself for his bravery and coolness. After having been in active service for a year or more, he returned to the United States to recruit his regiment. He was married in 1858 to a daughter of the Hon. Charles T. James of Providence. At the beginning of the rebellion, he was engaged with his father-in-law in the improvement, manufacture, and sale of the James cannon and projectiles. Appointed Major of the First Regiment, at the time of its enlistment, he at once exhibited military talent of no common order. His gallantry as a soldier at once secured our esteem, and his genial qualities, as a companion and friend, won our affections. On the 11th of May, Maj. Slocum left Washington for Rhode Island, for the purpose of raising the Second Regiment for the service for three years. He was appointed Colonel of this regiment upon its organization, and by his activity and energy, brought it to a high state of discipline. On the advance into Virginia, his regiment took the front of the column, and rendered great service in reconnoitering and as skirmishers. On the field, Col. Slocum fearlessly led his men into the thickest of the fight, with the words: "Now show them what Rhode Island can do,"—and, by the bravery of his example, assisted materially in the encouragement of our troops. He was shot early in the action, and fell, mortally wounded. He continued conscious but speechless, during the greater part of the day, but toward evening, fell into a comatose condition. He remained alive but insensible, till Tuesday, July 23, when he quietly breathed his last. I was with him a large part of the day of battle, and saw him a short time after he was struck. His face was calm and fair as in his brightest moments, and he met his death as a brave man should. Col. Burnside felt his loss most keenly, and speaks of him as an officer, whose career, had his life been spared, would have been most honorable to the State and the Nation.

HENRY A. PRESCOTT. I have already declared my appreciation of the high christian character and the brave and steady bearing of Lieut. Prescott. No braver or better man could be found in the ranks of the army of the Union. In the camp, his influence was always exercised for the benefit of his men, and of all who came within his reach. On the march, he was active, energetic, and enduring. On that Sunday morning, he frequently consulted his New Testament, which he always carried with him, seeking his strength in communion with his God. On the field, he was calm, collected, and fearless, leading the men of his company, until struck down by a bullet of the enemy, which took effect upon his forehead, killing him instantly. A true soldier of Jesus Christ, this man was; manly, honorable, high-minded, and devout—religious without pretence, and endowed with the courage that is born of duty and faith. He was born in Littleton, Mass., November 10, 1823. He was married to Miss Delia A. Graves, in Salem, Mass., in the spring of 1845. Removing to Providence, in February, 1850, he engaged in successful business, and soon gained the high esteem of all who knew his worth of character. An active and honored officer of the Providence Light Infantry Company, when the regiment was raised, he immediately volunteered. He regarded the service as of the most responsible duty, and, to him, the call to the field of strife, was like a call from Heaven. I have alluded to his work in the camp in the formation of a Christian Association. His religion was not a mere matter of form. The beauty and fidelity of his daily life proved the sincerity of his Christian profession, and became an influence of unspeakable good. The history of this war, rich as it may be in examples of virtue and Christian courage, will bear no brighter name, and furnish no better life than that of HENRY A. PRESCOTT.

LEVI TOWER.—In the death of Captain Tower, the State lost an officer who would have shed lustre upon its annals. He came of Revolutionary stock, his great-grandfather having been engaged in the war of Independence. His grandfather was an officer in the Newport corps of Artillery in the war of 1812. The young man inherited the courage and energy of his ancestors. He was born on the 18th day of August, 1835. He became a member of the Pawtucket Light Guard at the date of its formation in 1857, and rose from the ranks to the office of lieutenant. When the company was called to form a part of the 1st Regiment, he was chosen ensign, and served in that capacity during his connection with the Regiment. He was selected by Col. Burnside to command a detail of twenty-six men, who assisted in constructing and working a ferry from Georgetown to the Virginia side of the Potomac, which was used for the transportation of troops in the advance of May 23d. His faithfulness in this service recommended him to the attention of the authorities, and, in the formation of the 2d

Regiment he was offered and accepted a captaincy, June 1st. He was an excellent officer, and was strongly endeared to the men of his company, his friends and associates. He was killed while encouraging his company in the early part of the battle of Sunday, July 21st. The admirable qualities of his character made him always a favorite companion, and both our regiments mourned him as a beloved comrade. One of his friends writes as follows: "The best part of his story is his great kindness of heart, and it is this that makes his loss to his family so irreparable. He had a great love and reverence for aged persons, and was always seeking some means to minister to their happiness. He was also very susceptible to all moral and religious teachings, and was very faithful in all the trusts confided to him. He never wrote home without requesting our prayers for him." So writes one who knew him well, and we have here a glimpse of a beautiful and noble soul.

LIGHT BATTERY

BENJAMIN F. MARTINDALE was born in Western New York, 1833. When quite young he came to live in the family of Dr. Gideon Spencer, of Warwick, and spent his boyhood there. He served in a Massachusetts regiment in the Mexican war. He was a carpenter by trade, and also worked as a gas fitter. He was an active member of our battery, and returned with his company in August. He afterwards enlisted as corporal in the 1st Regiment of Light Artillery, and having joined the Burnside expedition, was killed while on picket duty, May 2d, 1862.

COMPANY A.

JAMES H. PECKHAM was a jeweler by occupation, and was, at the time of his death, 36 years of age. He was very highly esteemed for his manly and soldierly qualities by the men of his company. Appointed second sergeant of Company A, he was always active in the performance of his duty in that position.

Taken ill at Centreville, he did not accompany the regiment to the battle field. In the afternoon of Sunday, July 21st, finding that our army had been defeated, he attempted to make his way to Washington. He succeeded in reaching Georgetown, by way of Falls Church, but the fatigue of the journey, and the exposure of the night, were too much for his feeble strength, and he sank exhausted upon the door-stone of a dwelling in the streets of Georgetown. He was immediately taken into the house, and most kindly cared for by the inmates. His life ebbed rapidly away, and he died on Wednesday July 24th, 1861, sincerely lamented by his comrades. His remains were forwarded to Providence.

WARREN D. HAWKINS was born in Providence in the year 1837, and was a bootmaker by trade. He was an agreeable and intelligent companion, and proved himself a brave and faithful soldier. He was killed early in the action at Bull Run, on Sunday, July 21st, in the unflinching discharge of his duty.

HENRY H. LUTHER was born in Providence, and was a carpenter by occupation. A good soldier and brave man, he never shrank from any duty or danger, and fearlessly met a soldier's death on the battle field of Bull Run.

ANDREW J. WHITE was born in Millbury, Mass., in the year 1840. He was a machinist by occupation, and, joining the regiment at the time of its formation, did excellent service through the campaign. He was wounded at the battle of Bull Run, fell into the hands of the rebels, and died at Richmond, August 4th, 1861.

COMPANY B

THOMAS BOLTON was born in the city of Glocester, England, in the year 1834, and was a puddler by occupation. He was taken ill a short time previous to the departure of the regiment for Centreville, and died at the camp hospital, July 18th. He was a good soldier, and was much esteemed by his associates.

WILLARD CHAFFEE was born in Seekonk, Mass., in the year 1842, and was by occupation a machinist. He was a member of Co. B. in our regiment, and having creditably performed his duties there, he enlisted in the 3d Regiment at the time of its formation. He was killed in the battle of James Island, near Charleston, S. C., June 16th, 1862, having manifested in a most signal manner, his bravery as a soldier and his fidelity as a man.

COMPANY D.

JOHN R. ARNOLD was born in Providence, February 20th, 1837, and was by occupation a clerk. He became ill of typhoid fever, early in the month of July, and was unable to accompany the regiment on its march into Virginia. The disease was of a mild type, and he was supposed to be convalescent. He was removed from Washington on the 23d of July, and reached home on the 27th, but in making the journey he suffered a relapse, and died in Providence on the 30th day of July aged 24 years, 5 months and 10 days. He was a most worthy, faithful and conscientious young man, and, governed by a high sense of duty, freely offered his life for his country. His fine qualities of character attracted the respect of all who knew him, and the members of his company lamented, with genuine sorrow, the death of their comrade and friend.

JESSE COMSTOCK was born in Providence, February 11, 1843. He was educated in the public schools of the city. Upon his graduation from the High School, he entered into a counting room, intending to train himself for a mercantile life. He was active in all the duties of a soldier, bravely enduring the hardships and meeting the dangers of the campaign. He was wounded, just before the retreat, at the battle of Bull Run, and died at Sudley Church, July 31st, aged 18 years, 5 months and 20 days. His singular pure-mindedness, his affectionate disposition, and his warmth of heart, made him a universal favorite in the camp, and it was with profound sorrow that we left him to a sad and lingering death. A few of our number, who had been captured, watched his last days, and his dust sleeps undisturbed beneath the turf of the distant hill-side.

GEORGE W FLAGG was born in Providence in the year 1841. Impelled by a conscientious regard to the requirements of duty, he volunteered, among the first, to defend his country and its institutions. He was a very estimable young man, and a cool, self-possessed and fearless soldier. Mortally wounded at the battle of Bull Run, he was tenderly cared for during the day, though surgical aid was unavailing for his relief. He was taken prisoner on the retreat of our forces, and died at Gordonsville, August 3d, 1861. His friends have the consolation of knowing that he lived faithfully, and died submissively to the will of Providence. He was kindly treated by his captors, who communicated the intelligence of his decease to his afflicted family.

SAMUEL FOSTER passed through all the dangers of the campaign, and was unharmed in the battle of Bull Run. But on the retreat, he was missed by his company, and failed to reach the camp of the regiment, at Centreville. It is supposed that he was wounded, or killed, near the bridge across Cub Run, which was shelled by the rebel artillery. Though no tidings have ever been received of his fate, his friends still hope to hear that he is alive. He was a genial companion, a brave soldier and a dutiful man.

ALBERT B. PENNO was born in Providence, March 22, 1835. He was a bottler by occupation. He joined the regiment among the very first, and was a faithful and steady soldier. Severely wounded at the battle of Bull Run, on Sunday, July 21, he was taken prisoner at Sudley Church, and afterwards removed to Richmond, where he died August 4, 1861. He was a young man of good habits and correct principles, and held a high place in the regards of his associates.

THE DEAD.

COMPANY E.

FREDERICK DEXTER was born in Seekonk, Masssachusetts, in the year 1840. He was the only child of his parents, who thus, with ready patriotism, gave up the comfort and hope of their household. His father was a farmer in easy circumstances, and the young man enlisted in the company from Pawtucket under a pressing sense of duty to the cause. He creditably passed through his term of service, faithfully performing his duty. On his return home, he was taken ill of a severe typhoid fever, which terminated fatally on the 10th day of August, at his father's house at Cumberland. His funeral was attended by the members of Co. E, and a large number of friends, who thus attested their appreciation of his worth.

COMPANY F.

THOMAS J. HARRINGTON was born in Kerry County, Ireland, in the year 1837. He emigrated from his native country to America, and, upon removing to Newport, in 1858, became an operative in one of the manufacturing establishments of that city. He was a good citizen, and was esteemed by all who knew him for his correct and manly character. He joined Captain Tew's company and proved himself a good and efficient soldier. He was killed at the battle of Bull Run, July 21st, while bravely performing his duty to his adopted country.

THEODORE W. KING.*—Among the brave men who answered to the first call of the President of the United States for troops to defend the capital, and to stand by the Union, was Theodore Wheaton King, of whose brief life we make a short record. He was the youngest son of Dr. David King, and was born in Newport, R. I., in the year 1841. He went early to the private grammar schools of his native town. His tutor in French, mathematics, and in military exercise, at the school of the Rev.

---

*Communicated.

Mr. Leverett, was M. Vigier de Monteuil, who fell at the battle of Roanoke Island. The last two years were passed at Phillips' Academy, Andover, The breaking out of the rebellion found him at Andover. On learning that South Carolina had seceded, he wrote to a friend that if the South attempted to destroy the Union, he should consider it his duty to pour out his blood to the last drop for his country. The fall of Sumter, and the summons of the President, fixed his decision; and, at Providence, while on his way to school at Andover, he enlisted as a private in Company F. He went with the first detachment of five hundred men, and encountered the difficulties and dangers that beset them between Annapolis and Washington. As a soldier he was ever ready for the performance of duty; ever desirous to join any party selected for the accomplishment of difficult and important tasks. On the night of the 20th of July, he was very ill from fatigue and exhaustion. He was placed in the hospital at Centreville, but, hearing that his regiment had passed on, he rose from his bed, and, armed with his gun and revolver, followed rapidly, until he overtook his company, saying to his companions, who were surprised at seeing him, knowing that an hour before he was very ill—"No man shall say that I failed in my duty." When the regiment was ordered into action, he marched boldly to the front, and fought bravely until he fell, struck by a Minie ball, which shattered his thigh bone. Left by his retreating companions in arms, he was taken at night into a shanty near by, where Col. Slocum and Maj. Ballou, of his own brigade, were dying. A fortnight of suffering was passed here, lying on the floor, with no proper dressing of his wound. He was carried thence to Richmond. Four months he passed in the Richmond tobacco warehouse, or prison hospital. His constitution was gradually undermined, by the suppuration of his wound, the pestiferous atmosphere, the imperfect diet, and the want of necessary stimulants. One or two friends of his parents visited him in prison, and offered him succor, which, from delicacy, he refused.

By his calm, patient endurance of suffering, and his mild, amiable temper, he won the regard of the surgeon of the hospital, Dr. Eden Higginbotham, who made his best efforts to save him, and who finally took him to his own house, where his parents found him when they reached Richmond, about the middle of December, 1861. When his father reached him at Richmond, his body was emaciated to an extreme degree, but his voice was clear and unaltered, and his mind calm, firm and hopeful. This hopeful state continued while delayed at Richmond, and at Fortress Monroe. On his arrival at Philadelphia, he was taken to the hospitable mansion of Clement C. Barclay, Esq., for the purpose of recruiting his strength to bear the journey home. Here, notwithstanding the assiduities of the kindest friends, the efforts of the most skillful physicians and surgeons, the best wishes of a deeply-sympathizing community, and the prayers of the true, the good, and the faithful, he gradually sunk into the repose of death, on the morning of January 28, 1862. He was distinguished for a love of nature, refinement of mind and heart, coolness and self-possession in the hour of danger, and fidelity in every scene of duty. A brave and heautiful youth, his name will long be cherished by his friends, as one who gave up all for his country, his duty, and his God.

JOHN P. PECKHAM was born in Newport, Aug. 22, 1841, and was a carpenter by trade. He was a young man of excellent character; was always an obedient child, an attendant at Sunday School, and about six months before he left Newport with the regiment, he joined the Marlborough Street Methodist Episcopal Church. His character was always most exemplary, and he was universally beloved by all who knew him. He volunteered as a religious and patriotic duty. A member of the gallant color company, he bravely did his work as a man and soldier, and, by his death, added another name to the list of those who have been "slain for the testimony which they held." He was killed at the battle of Bull Run, July 21, 1861, and his memory is gratefully preserved by his surviving comrades.

COMPANY G.

PAUL DOWNES was born in Lancashire, England, in 1833, and was consequently 28 years of age at the time of his death. He removed to this country and engaged in the business of a machinist. He was wounded in the battle of Bull Run, July 21, and was captured by the enemy. He died at Richmond, Aug. 1, 1861. He was a brave man and a good soldier.

HERMAN SCHOCKER was a native of Saxony, and was born in the year 1816. A few years since, with his wife and family, he removed to this country. He was a jeweller by occupation, and his fidelity and industry secured for him the confidence of his employers. An ardent lover of free institutions, and an intelligent citizen, when his adopted country was threatened with destruction, he hastened to enroll himself in the ranks of her defenders. He had crossed the seas for the sake of living in a free country, and he appreciated the worth of liberty. He passed through the campaign with credit to himself, and was killed while fighting for the cause which he loved.

DANIEL LYMAN ARNOLD was the youngest son of the late Governor Lemuel H. Arnold, of this State, and brother in-law of Brigadier General I. P. Rodman, of South Kingstown. His maternal grandfather, Colonel Daniel Lyman, figured conspicuously in the Revolution, and subsequently in the political history of Rhode Island. He was born in the year 1831. He enlisted in the 1st Regiment, at the time of its formation, as a private, and was promoted to Corporal, for gallantry at the battle of Bull Run. He remained at home, after the return of the Regiment, till January, 1862, when he received the appointment of Sergeant in the 3d Regiment. He faithfully performed his duty at Port Royal, and accompanied the battalion which joined the expedition against Charleston. He was mortally wounded at the battle of James Island, June 16th, 1862, and died on Tuesday, June 24th.

COMPANY H.

JAMES DOUGHERTY was a native of Ireland. He was born in Tyrone, in the year 1837, and was a jeweller by trade. Entering the ranks of the army, he faithfully performed his allotted work, and met his fate at the battle of Bull Run, July 21, 1861. For the country which had befriended him as an exile, he was willing to give his life. Our adopted citizens have nobly performed their full share of the perilous work which the times demanded, and in their annals, this humble name will not be forgotten.

JOHN FALVEY was born in Providence, in the year 1843, and followed the occupation of a barber. He was a young man of genial qualities of character, and of ready wit. On the march to Centreville, he was overcome by fatigue, and, when the regiment marched to Bull Run, he remained in the camp. Falling into the hands of the enemy, after the retreat, he rapidly became ill, and died at Richmond, on the 28th day of July, 1861.

COMPANY I.

ALBERT H. BURDICK was born in Genesee county, N. Y., in the year 1837, and was a machinist by occupation. Company I was one of the best companies in the regiment, as attested by the official despatches of Col. Burnside, and private Burdick well sustained the credit of his company. He was mortally wounded at Bull Run, and probably died soon after the day of the battle.

SAMUEL C. DANFORTH was a native of Saco, Maine, and was a laborer by occupation. He was born in the year 1843, and was among the youngest men of his company. But, though so young, he was among the most active and efficient, and deserves honorable mention among those whose courage has given glory to our State. He was killed at the battle of Bull Run, July 21, 1861.

APPENDIX C.

HENRY H. REMINGTON was born in East Greenwich, R. I., in the year 1842. He passed through all the experiences of the campaign with credit to himself. But after the disbandment of the regiment, he was taken seriously ill, and died at Providence, August 28, 1861. He was a young man of correct habits, and secured, by his quiet fidelity, the regard of his associates.

COMPANY K.

WILLIAM H. ACKLEY was born at White Creek, N. Y., in the year 1827, and was a farmer by occupation. He joined the regiment when Company K was first enlisted, and was employed as wagoner. He honorably passed through the dangers of the campaign, and in creditable contrast to many others, drove his wagon into Washington in safety, bringing in several wounded men. The fatigue and exposure to which he was subjected produced severe illness and prostration, from which he could not rally. He died, July 24, at the Regimental Hospital in Washington, and was buried, according to military usage, in Glenwood Cemetery.

ERASMUS S. BARTHOLOMEW was born in Denmark, N. Y., in the year 1831, and followed the occupation of a dentist in the village of Woonsocket, at the time of the organization of the First Regiment. He joined Company K, and was appointed first corporal. After the disbandment of the First Regiment, he joined Capt. Tourtelotte's company in the Third Regiment, with the rank of sergeant. His admirable qualities as a man and soldier attracted the commendation of·his superior officers, and he was soon appointed acting Sergeant Major of the regiment. Here, too, he received great praise, and on the 21st day of May, 1862, he was commissioned as Lieutenant, and assigned to Company E. He was mortally wounded in the battle of James Island, June 16, 1862, and died on the following day. During his connection with the First Regiment, he commanded the esteem of all by the genuineness of his religious character, and the sincerity of his life. Engaged for a time in the hospital, he was most assiduous in the care and attention which he bestowed upon the sick, and by the cheerfulness, kindness, and diligence which he brought to this office, conduced greatly to the comfort of the patients and the alleviation of their pain. His former and his more recent comrades speak equally in his favor, and his death must be an afflictive bereavement to his fellow officers, and a severe loss to the entire regiment.

HENRY C. DAVIS was a member of the company from Woonsocket, and enlisted from motives of sincere patriotism. Hardly capable of enduring the hardships of a soldier's life, he became ill soon after the Regiment went into camp, and died in the hospital, June 16, 1861, while the Regiment was absent on the expedition towards Harper's Ferry. His funeral obsequies were attended by Father Quinn, and a Baptist clergyman from the city of Washington, and his body sent to Woonsocket for interment.

JOSEPH HARROP was born at Ossett, Ireland, in the year 1837, and was employed as a weaver at the time of the commencement of the rebellion. He was a faithful soldier, and well performed his part in the work of the army. He was killed at the battle of Bull Run, July 21, 1861.

HUGH MELVILLE was born in the town of Groton., Vermont, in the year 1821, and was a blacksmith by trade. He was a brave soldier in the Mexican war, and when the rebellion broke out, he at once took arms again to defend the institutions and laws of the country. He is declared to have been, in all positions, an active, courageous, and dutiful soldier. Killed at Bull Run, in the early part of the battle of July 21, his memory is cherished by his late comrades, and held in grateful esteem by all who knew the humble fidelity of his life.

MATTHEW QUIRK was born at Clomwell, Ireland, in the year 1816. Removing to this country, he found employment as a laborer. When the war began, he enlisted in Company K, and after faithful service, was killed in battle, July 21, 1861.

GEORGE J. HILL was born at Upton, Mass. in the year 1833, and was by occupation a shoemaker. He was an excellent member of Company K, and faithfully performed all the duties of his position while connected with the First Regiment. Upon the formation of the Third Regiment he enlisted in Company D, and received the appointment of Sergeant. He was present at the siege of Fort Pulaski, and when that post was repossessed by the United States forces, his company formed a portion of the garrison. He was mortally wounded by the accidental explosion of a shell in the fort on the 14th day of April 1862, and soon after died.

POSTSCRIPT.—HENRY E. TESTEN was a native of Massachusetts, having been born in Blackstone, in the year 1843. He was a member of Co. G., in our regiment, and was a good soldier. He enlisted in Battery C., 1st Regiment Light Artillery, in the Autumn of 1861, and was killed in battle in front of Richmond, June 27, 1862.

APPENDIX D

ROLL OF THE REGIMENT.

In making up the Roll of the Regiment, I have placed opposite the names of the officers and men, in the greater number of instances, the positions which they filled, July 1, 1862. The dates of the enlistments and appointments are necessarily imperfectly ascertained, as they extend over the time between the organization and departure of the regiments to which the officers and men were attached. In some instances the enlistments and appointments were made after the departure of the regiments. I therefore am obliged to be contented with giving the dates as below:

3d Regiment R. I. V., organized Aug. 12, 1861, left Providence Sept 7, 1861, and was enlarged to 12 companies, Feb. 1862.

4th Regiment R. I. V., organized Aug. 15, 1861, left Providence Oct. 5, 1861.

5th Regiment R. I. V., organized Oct. 1861, left Providence as a battalion of five companies, Dec. 27, 1861.

1st Regiment R. I. Cavalry, (eight companies from Rhode Island, four companies from New Hampshire), organized Oct. 1861, left Providence March 8, 1862.

1st Regiment R. I. L. A., organized Sept. 13, 1861, left Providence as the batteries were filled, to Jan., 1862.

7th Regiment R. I. V., organized, in part, May, 1862.

The 9th and 10th Regiments, with a Battery, were raised for three months service, and left for Washington on the 27th–29th of May, 1862.

The 7th Squadron of Cavalry, (one company from Rhode Island, one company from New Hampshire and Vermont), was also raised for three months, and left for Washington on the 26th day of June, 1862.

FIELD AND STAFF OFFICERS.

Colonel, AMBROSE E. BURNSIDE. Brigadier General of Volunteers, U. S. A., Aug. 6, 1861; Major General, March 18th, 1862. In command of the Department of North Carolina.*

Lieutenant Colonel, JOSEPH S. PITMAN.

First Major, JOHN S. SLOCUM, resigned, and appointed Colonel of 2d Regiment R. I. V., May 8th. 1861. Mortally wounded in the battle of Bull Run, July 21st, and died July 23d, 1861.

First Major, JOSEPH P. BALCH, promoted from 2d Major June 27, 1861.

Second Major, WILLIAM GODDARD, appointed June 27th, 1861.

Surgeon, FRANCIS L. WHEATON; resigned, and appointed Surgeon in 2d Regiment R. I. V., June 6, 1861. Brigade Surgeon.

Surgeon, HENRY W. RIVERS, promoted from Assistant Surgeon, June 7th. Surgeon 4th Regiment R. I. V.; promoted to Brigade Surgeon, March, 1862.

Assistant Surgeon, NATHANIEL MILLER.

Assistant Surgeon, GEORGE W. CARR. Appointed Assistant Surgeon in 2d Regiment R. I. V., August 27th, 1861.

Assistant Surgeon, JAMES HARRIS, attached to 2d Regiment, July 1st, 1861; taken prisoner at the battle of Bull Run,

---

*Robert Holloway was the colored servant of Col. Burnside, and was most devotedly attached to him. He had received great kindness at Col. B's hands, while that officer was serving in New Mexico, in 1850, and followed him to the East. He had the misfortune of being captured at the battle of Bull Run, but was released early in March, 1862, and immediately joined General Burnside at Newbern, N. C.

ROLL OF THE REGIMENT. 171

July 21st; released September, 1861. Appointed Superintendent of the United States Hospital at Providence, April, 1862.

Adjutant, CHARLES H. MERRIMAN.* Appointed Major of 10th Regiment R. I. V., May 26th, 1862; resigned June, 1862.

Quartermaster, CYRUS G. DYER, resigned, and appointed Captain in 2d Regiment R. I. V., June 5th, 1861.

Quartermaster, WM. LLOYD BOWERS; promoted from Commissary, June 5th, 1861; taken prisoner at the battle of Bull Run, July 21st; released, and returned to Providence, January 25th, 1862.

Commissary, ALVAN COLE.

Paymaster, HENRY T. SISSON. Appointed Captain, December 20th, 1861, and promoted to Major 3d Regiment R. I. H. A., February 5th, 1862.

Chaplain, AUGUSTUS WOODBURY.

Assistant Chaplain, THOMAS QUINN. Appointed Chaplain 3d Regiment R. I. H. A.; transferred to 1st Regiment R. I. L. A.; discharged January 8th, 1862.

Engineer, HENRY A. DEWITT, promoted from private May 31st.

Nativities of Field and Staff were as follows: Rhode Island 11; Indiana, 1; Massachusetts, 1; not returned, 5. Taken prisoners, 2.

NON COMMISSIONED STAFF

Sergeant Major, JOHN P. SHAW; resigned and appointed Lieutenant in 2d Regiment R. I. V., June 6th, 1861.

Sergeant Major, JOHN S. ENGS, promoted from private, June 8th.

---

* When Colonel Burnside was appointed to the command of his Brigade, Adjutant Merriman was appointed Acting Assistant Adjutant General and Chief of the Staff, and admirably performed his duties in every position. His office in the Regiment itself was most laborious and responsible, and was filled in the most acceptable manner. He received the highest commendation at the Head Quarters of the Army, for the accuracy of his returns, and the general fidelity of his work.

APPENDIX D.

Quartermaster's Sergeant, HENRY A. BARTLETT, relieved May 2d. Appointed Lieutenant U. S. Marine Corps.
Quartermaster's Sergeant, ELIAS M. JENCKES.
Commissary Sergeant, WILLIAM L. HUNTER.
Ordnance Sergeant, JAMES W. LYON. Lieutenant in 4th Regiment, R. I. V.
Drum Major, BENJAMIN G. WEST. Bugler in 3d Regiment R. I. H. A.
Hospital Steward, JAMES H. TAYLOR.
Nativities: Rhode Island, 8.

THE REGIMENTAL BAND

The American Brass Band, of Providence, patriotically volunteered, immediately upon the outbreak of hostilities, to accompany the regiment. It is unnecessary to comment upon the invaluable services which its members rendered in the camp, on the march, and upon the battle-field in the care of the wounded and dying. Always prompt, ready and generous, the Band, under the inimitable direction of its veteran leader, added to its already high reputation, and won the highest encomiums of all listeners to its music.

Joseph C. Greene, Band Master. Band Master 4th Reg. R. I. V.
Henry L. Dana. In band at Naval School, Newport.
Alfred E. Dickerson.
William L. Dunbar.
Thomas P. Fenner. In band at Naval School, Newport.
John C. Harrington.
Willard Haskell. In band at Naval School, Newport.
Augustus Heise.
William W Hall.
Walter B. Kingsley. In band at Naval School, Newport.
George E. Mason.
William F. Marshall. Band Master in 3d Regiment R. I. H. A; resigned May, 1862, and appointed Director of Band at Naval School, Newport, June, 1862.

ROLL OF THE REGIMENT. 173

Emery Paine.
Abijah M. Pond.
Edward L. Potter.
Carroll J. Pullen.
William Lee Reynolds.
Beriah G. Reynolds.
Samuel D. Spink,
Stephen R. Sweet.
Sylvester J. Sweet.
William E. Whiting.
Stephen G. Whittemore.

The nativities of the Band were as follows: Rhode Island, 15; Massachusetts, 3; Maine, 1; Connecticut, 1; New York, 1; England, 1; Germany, 1; not returned, 1. Total, 24.

The Band has furnished 2 Band Masters, and 4 members of Band, U. S. N.

BATTERY OF LIGHT ARTILLERY.*

Charles H. Tompkins, Captain. Appointed Colonel 1st Regiment R. I. L. A., September 13th, 1861.
William H. Reynolds, 1st Lieutenant. Resigned, June 1st; appointed Captain in 2d Battery R. I. L. A.; promoted, September 13th, 1861, to Lieut. Colonel, 1st Regiment R. I. L. A.; appointed Government Agent at Port Royal, S. C.; resigned, June 26th, 1862.
Benjamin F. Remington, Jr., 2d Lieutenant. Promoted to 1st Lieutenant June 1st.
Augustus M. Tower, 3d Lieutenant. Promoted to 2d Lieutenant, June 1st.

---

* This was the first battery of rifled cannon in the service of the United States, either volunteer or regular.

Henry B. Brastow, 4th Lieutenant. Promoted to 3d Lieutenant, June 1st. Assistant Government Agent at Port Royal; resigned June, 1862.

Charles H. Pope, 4th Lieutenant. Appointed from 1st Sergeant, June 1st. Lieutenant 1st Regiment R. I. L. A.

Walter O. Bartlett, Staff Sergeant. Captain in 1st Regiment R. I. L. A.

Thomas F. Vaughan, First Sergeant. Appointed Lieutenant in 2d Battery R. I. L. A. June 7th, 1861; promoted to Captain August 21st, 1861; resigned December 11, 1861; appointed Captain of an Illinois battery, June, 1862.

George C. Harkness, Second Sergeant. Lieutenant in 1st Regiment R. I. L. A.

William W Pearce, Third Sergeant.

Edwin C. Gallup, Fourth Sergeant. Captain in volunteer battery, for three months' service, May 26th, 1862.

Henrie Crandall, Fifth Sergeant.

George C. DeMarini, Sixth Sergeant.

Stephen W. Fisk, First Corporal. Lieutenant 1st Regiment R. I. L. A,

Frank G. Allen, Second Corporal.

James S. Davis, Jr., Third Corporal. Sergeant in volunteer battery for three months, May 26th, 1862.

J. Henry Wilbur, Jr., Fourth Corporal.

Thomas Simpson, Fifth Corporal. Lieut. 1st Reg't R. I. L. A.

E. P. Butts, Jr., Sixth Corporal.

Walter H. Wild, Seventh Corporal. Bugler 3d Regiment R. I. H. A.

Richmond Henshaw, Eighth Corporal. Lieutenant in a New York artillery regiment.

William W. Pearce, Ninth Corporal.

Henry W. Brown, Tenth Corporal. Sergeant in volunteer Battery for three months' service, May 26th, 1861.

ROLL OF THE REGIMENT. 175

Calvin J. Adams Eleventh Corporal. Sergeant in volunteer battery for three months, May 26th, 1862.
B. F. Worsley, Twelfth Corporal.
Gilbert B. Dana, First Bugler.
George W. Fuller, Second Bugler.
William Elsbree, First Artificer.
William Bachelder, Second Artificer.
Benjamin N. Whipple, Third Artificer. Artificer 1st Regiment R. I. L. A.
James B. Peck, Fourth Artificer.
H. R. Gladding, Fifth Artificer. Lieut. 1st Reg't R. I. L. A.
C. H. Scrutton, Sixth Artificer.
Joseph Watson, First Guidon.
Charles H. Adams. Sergeant 1st Regiment R. I. L. A.
George W. Adams. Lieut. in 1st Regiment R. I. L. A.
Albert F. Allen.
James Allen. Aeronaut, with Professor Lowe.
Edwin E. Anthony.
William R. Arnold.
Walter Arnold. Private in 1st Regiment R. I. L. A.
William Brophey. Sergeant in 3d Regiment R. I. H. A.
Edward F. Bacon.
J. Manton Bradley.
D. S. Barney.
Allen A. Blackington.
George W Blair. Sergeant in 1st Regiment R. I. L. A.
J. C. Bogues.
Joseph T. Bosworth. Private in 1st Regiment R. I. L. A.
Edwin F Brown.
William Beiswanger.
Otis P. Bucklin.
Edward F. Budlong. Private in 1st Regiment R. I. L. A.
Horace S. Bloodgood. Lieut. in 1st Regiment R. I. L. A.
George W. Cowden.
Thomas Conway.

James Comins. Private in 1st Regiment R. I. C.
Richard Cronan,
Constantine Cokeley.
Matthew Conley.
Albert Daggett.
Reuben D. Dodge. Sergeant in 1st Regiment R. I. L. A.
Daniel C. Dore. Private in 1st Regiment R. I. L. A.
William S. Dyer. Quartermaster's Sergeant in 1st Regiment R. I. L. A.
Daniel Earle. Sergeant in a New York Artillery Regiment.
Charles C. Eldridge Sergeant in 1st Regiment R. I. L. A.
Charles R. Farnum.
George E. Fiske.
Jeremiah Fitzgerald. Sergeant in 1st Regiment R. I. C.
Joseph G. Fowler.
Benjamin W. Foster.
F J. Garbanati. Lieut. in a New York Artillery regiment.
Thomas G. Glover.
Edward Goddard. Sergeant in 1st Reg't R. I. L. A.; deserted.
George C. Greene.
Smith Greene, discharged July 8th. Private in 1st Regiment R. I. L. A.; discharged May, 1862.
Charles E. Guild. Sergeant in 1st Regiment R. I. L. A.
H. A. Guild. Corporal in volunteer battery for three months, May 26th, 1862.
Charles C. Gray.
John Geloghly. Private in 1st Regiment R. I. L. A.
James M. Grosvenor.
William Hennessy.
Jabob Haggadorn. Lieutenant in 7th Regiment R. I. V., July 1862.
George Hammond. Sergeant in 1st Regiment R. I. L. A.
George W. Helwig. Sergeant in a New York Artillery Reg't.
John F. Horton.
Christian Hock.

ROLL OF THE REGIMENT.

John Irwin.
Henry P. Jordon.
Michael Kenney. Private in 1st Regiment R. I. L. A.
Patrick Kenney.
Charles Kimball. Artificer in 1st Regiment R. I. L. A.
Thomas B. Kimball.
Charles H. Kennison. Sergeant 1st Regiment R. I. L. A.
B D. G. Levalley.
Stephen D. Lockwood. Discharged in May, 1861. Private in 2d Regiment R. I. V
Richard Loughman.
B. F. Martindale. Corporal in 1st Regiment R. I. L. A.; killed at Newbern, May 2d, 1862.
E. H. Matteson. Sergeant in 1st Regiment R. I. L. A.
James T. Mauran. Private 1st Regiment R. I. L. A.
S. M. Maybury.
C. H. V. Mayo. Private 1st Regiment R. I. L. A.
Patrick McElroy.
Rufus Miller. Private 3d Regiment R. I. H. A.
William Millen. Sergeant 1st Regiment R. I. L. A.
John McLoughlin. Hostler with the Burnside expedition.
Jeremiah Murphy.
Thomas E. Noonan. Private in 10th Regiment R. I. V., (three months).
Ellery B. Northup. Farrier in volunteer battery for three months, May 26th, 1862.
William A. Nye.
Manuel Otis. Private 1st Regiment R. I. L. A.
George W. Paton.
Raymond H. Perry. Lieutenant in 1st Regiment R. I. L. A.
Thomas R. Phinney.
J. W Razee. Private in 1st Regiment R. I. L. A.
John B. Remlinger. Corporal in volunteer battery, (three months), May 26th, 1862.
Reuben H. Rich. Sergeant in 1st Regiment R. I. L. A.

APPENDIX D.

D. G. Ross. Private in 3d Regiment R. I. H. A.
Philander Robbins. Private in 7th Regiment R. I. V.
Hugh Rider. Private 1st Regiment R. I. L. A.
George O. Scott.
George F. Seaver. Lieutenant in 3d Regiment R. I. H. A.
Lothrop B. Shurtleff. Sergeant in 1st Regiment R. I. C.
George H. Smith. Corporal in 1st Regiment R. I. L. A.
Byron D. Snow. Private 1st Regiment R. I. L. A.
James Sweeney.
William K. Sweet. Private in 1st Regiment R. I. L. A.
J. W. Stone. Private in 7th Regiment R. I. V.
Henry Smith.
Ernest Staples. Lieutenant in a New York artillery regiment.
Charles G. Taft. Sergeant 1st Regiment R. I. L. A.
William Thornley. Artificer 1st Regiment R. I. L. A.
Ziba C. Thayer. Hostler in 1st Regiment R. I. L. A.
Olney Trainer. Private 1st Regiment R. I. L. A.
Joseph E. Tulley.
William L. Tyrrell. Corporal in volunteer battery for three months, May 26, 1862.
James D. Van Amringer.
William H. Walcott. Discharged June 7th, and appointed Lieutenant in 2d Battery R. I. L. A. Resigned, and appointed Lieutenant in 17th Infantry, U. S. A., commission dating May 14, 1861.
Richard Waterman. Lieutenant in 1st Regiment R. I. L. A.
John Warcham. Corporal in 1st Regiment R. I. L. A.
George B. Warfield. Private in 1st Regiment R. I. C.
Charles H. Wilcox. Sergeant in 1st Regiment R. I L. A.
John G. Williams. Wagoner 1st Regiment R. I. L. A.
James E. Wood. Private in 1st Regiment R. I. C.
Frederic Woodward. Sergeant in 1st Regiment R. I. C.

The nativities of this company were as follows: Rhode Island, 55; Massachusetts, 30; New York, 9; Connecticut 4;

ROLL OF THE REGIMENT. 179

Maine, 4 ; Pennsylvania, 3 ; New Hampshire, 2 ; Maryland, 1 ; Virginia, 1 ; Ireland, 14 ; Germany, 6 ; England, 3 ; France, 1 ; Cuba, 1 ; not returned, 12. Total officers and men, 146. Average age 26 years. Oldest man, 52 ; youngest, 18. Average height, 5 feet, 7 3-8 inches.

This company has furnished for the war, 1 Colonel, 1 Lieut. Colonel,* 2 Captains, 13 Lieutenants, 20 Sergeants,† 3 Artificers, 3 corporals, 1 Assistant Government Agent,* 1 Bugler, 23 Privates,† 1 Wagoner, and 2 Hostlers; to the United States army, 1 Lieutenant, and to the volunteer service for three months, 1 Captain, 3 Sergeants, 4 Corporals, 1 Private, and 1 Farrier. JAMES ALLEN was joined to this company as an Aeronaut ; is now employed in the same capacity with Professor Lowe, and is connected with Gen. M:Clellan's army.

COMPANY A

Arthur F. Dexter, Captain. Appointed Captain on Staff of Brig. Gen. Tyler, April, 1862; afterwards resigned.
Addison H. White, 1st Lieutenant.
Frank G. Low, 2d Lieutenant. Captain in 10th Regiment R. I. V., three months.
Charles W. Topliff, Ensign.
Thomas B. Briggs, First Sergeant. Captain in 3d Regiment R. I. H. A.
James H. Peckham, Second Sergeant. Died July 24, 1861, of disease of the heart.
Joseph T. P. Bucklin, Third Sergeant. Captain in 4th Regiment R. I. V.
Manson H. Najac, Fourth Sergeant. Sergeant 9th Regiment, three months.
Edwin L. Cook, First Corporal.

---

* Resigned. † 1 Sergeant, 1 Private, discharged. 1 Sergeant deserted.

Sylvester Marvel, Second Corporal.   Sergeant in 3d Regiment R. I. H. A.
Chester L. Turner, Third Corporal.
William H. French, Fourth Corporal.   Clerk with Major General Burnside.
Michael Gallagher, Musician.   Private in 1st Regiment R. I. C.
Benjamin L. Hall, Musician.   Appointed Sergeant November, 1861, and promoted to Lieutenant 5th Regiment R. I. V., May, 1862.
Thomas J. Abbott, Jr.
William C. Almy.
Lyman Arnold.   Lieutenant in a regiment of Conn. volunteers.
William B. Avery.   Lieutenant in Naval Brigade, General Burnside's Expedition.
William F. Baldwin.
Daniel Barney.
Otis A. Baker.   Wounded in the battle of Bull Run, July 21, 1861.   Lieutenant in 4th Regiment R. I. V.
Charles E. Beers.   Commissary Sergeant in 5th Reg't R. I. V.
John G. Beveridge.   Lieutenant in 2d Regiment R. I. V
James E. Blackmer.   Sergeant in 9th Regiment R. I. V., three months.
Jabez B. Blanding.   Lieutenant in 3d Regiment R. I. H. A.
George F. Boyden.
Amos M. Bowen.   Taken prisoner at Bull Run, July 21st; released May, 1862.
Lucius W. Bonney.   In U. S. Navy.
Joseph R. Bullock.
Whipple B. Bradley.
Edwin Burgess.
James E. Burke,
Charles W. Brown.
John B. Campbell.   Sergeant of Carbineers, June 27.   Lieut. in 26th Regiment Massachusetts Volunteers.   Res'd.
John K. Chace, Jr.

ROLL OF THE REGIMENT. 181

Ezra C. Colvin. In U. S. Navy.
Patrick Crawley. In U. S. Navy.
George Curtis. Lieutenant in 4th Regiment R. I. V
George W Cushing, Jr., Clerk in Treasury Department, Washington.
George K. Davis.
James F. Davison. Private in 9th Regiment R. I. V., three months.
William P. Dean. Scout with Gen. Burnside's expedition.
Charles E. Douglass. Sergeant in 5th Regiment R. I. V.
James H. Earle.
John J. Field. Sergeant in 3d Regiment R. I. H. A.
William Galliger. Broke his leg on march from Annapolis.
William H. Gardiner. Sergeant in 1st Regiment R. I. C.
Thomas J. A. Gross.
William F. Green.
Henry F. Green.
Albert Griggs.
Thomas J. Griffin. Detailed for Hospital service. Hospital Steward in 4th Regiment R. I. V.
Charles C. Harris. Sergeant Major in 1st Regiment R. I. C.
Daniel Harris. Discharged May, 1861.
Warren D. Hawkins. Killed in the battle of Bull Run, July 21st.
James H. Irving.
Henry M. James.
William H. Jay. Corporal in 3d Regiment R. I. H. A.
William C. Johnson.
Cornelius Keif.
Samuel R. Keenan. Discharged May 31st. Sergeant in a Massachusetts Regiment.
Winslow B. Kent. Mustered June 20th.
James Lake. Mustered June 3d. Master's Mate U. S. N.
Charles S. Langley.

Herbert A. Lewis. Sergeant in 3d Regiment R. I. II. A. Wounded in battle of Bull Run, July 21st, 1861.
Cyrus W. Lindsey. Wounded in battle of Bull Run, July 21st, 1861.
Frank A. Lucas.
Henry H. Luther. Killed in the battle of Bull Run, July 21st.
Edward E. Mason.
Samuel P. Mason. Comm. Sergeant in 1st Regiment R. I. C.
James A. Manchester. Sergeant in 9th Regiment (three months)
Thomas Manchester. Quartermaster's Sergeant in 1st Regiment R. I. C.
William McCall.
Edwin Maguire.
Sylvanus Martin. Discharged July 3d. Private in 9th Regiment R. I. V., three months.
John F. Morris. Corporal in 4th Regiment R. I. V.
Charles E. Murray.
Frederic N. Padelford.
Christopher Pearce.
Duncan A. Pell. Captain, Aide de Camp to Major General Burnside.
Henry W. Phillips.
Harrison W Potter. Private 9th Reg't R. I. V., three months.
John Randolph.
George C. Rhodes.
Samuel E. G. Richards. Sergeant in 5th Regiment R. I. V.
Joseph B. Ripley.
Josiah W. Robinson, Jr., Sergeant in Regiment R. I. H. A.
Nathan A. Smith.
James A. Smith. Sergeant in 1st Regiment R. I. C.
Charles W. Snow.
John E. Snow. Captain in 5th Regiment R. I. V.
Samuel Spink.
James F. Sweet.
Edward D. Sweetland.

William E. Taber, Jr. Captain 10th Regiment R. I. V., three months.
Benjamin Tallman. Private in 1st Regiment R. I. C.
Randall H. Tallman. Scout in General Burnside's expedition.
John W. Tate.
Alexander T. Taylor. Private in 2d Regiment R. I. V.
George O. Taylor.
William A. J. Thayer.
Josiah Thornton. Private in 3d Regiment R. I. H. A.
Solomon Thornton.
Albert G. Tillinghast. Sergeant in 4th Regiment R. I. V.
Henry L. Tillinghast. Died February 25th, 1862.
Franklin P Tompkins. Sergeant 4th Regiment R. I. V.
Pardon Vaughan.
Albert Weaver. Corporal in 3d Regiment R. I. H. A.
Andrew J. White. Wounded and taken prisoner at Bull Run, July 21st, 1861. Died at Richmond, August 4th.
William Wilson. Wagoner in 4th Regiment R. I. V.
Nathan Winslow.

The nativities of this company were as follows: Rhode Island, 62; Massachusetts, 17; Connecticut, 3; Maine, 2; Ireland, 2; New York, 1; New Jersey, 1; New Hampshire, 1; Illinois, 1; Scotland, 1; not returned, 18.

Total, officers and men, 109.

Killed, 2; wounded, taken prisoner, and since died, 4; died in service, 1; taken prisoner, 1.

Average age, 25 years. Oldest man, 41; youngest, 18.

Average height, 5 feet, 7 1-2 inches.

This company has furnished for the war, 2 Captains, A. D. C.; 3 Captains in the line; 9 Lieutenants; 1 Sergeant Major; 14 Sergeants; 3 Corporals; 1 Hospital Steward; 1 Clerk to MajorGeneral; 2 Scouts; 1 Wagoner; 4 Privates; 1 Lieutenant Naval Brigade; 1 Master's Mate, U. S. N.; 3 Sailors U. S. N. And for three months' service, 2 Captains, 3 Sergeants; and 3 Privates.

COMPANY B.

Nicholas Van Slyck, Captain. Appointed Lieutenant Colonel 9t Regiment R. I. V., three months, May 26th 1862. Afterwards resigned.

Nelson Viall, First Lieutenant. Resigned, June 4th, and appointed Captain in 2d Regiment R. I. V Promoted to Major after the battle of Bull Run. Promoted to Lieutenant Colonel, June 25th, 1862.

James E. Bailey, Second Lieutenant. Promoted to 1st Lieut. June 4th. Captain in 3d Regiment R. I. H. A.

James R. Holden, Second Lieutenant. Promoted from 1st Sergeant June 4th.. Captain 9th Regiment R. I. V., three months.

James E. Hidden, Ensign. Resigned June 9th.

John D. Eldridge, First Sergeant. Promoted from 3d Corporal, June 4th. Captain 3d Reg't R. I. H. A. Res'd.

Silas A. Winchester, Second Sergeant. Resigned, June 30th.

Jason A. Blackmar, Second Sergeant. Promoted from 3d Sergeant, June 30th.

Thomas Connor, Third Sergeant. Promoted from 2d Corporal, June 30th.

Augustus S. Randall, Fourth Sergeant. Discharged July 8th.

Benjamin R. Gurney, First Corporal.

Henry F. Streeter, Second Corporal. Promoted from Private June 30th.

James A. Seaver, Third Corporal. Discharged May 31st. Sergeant 3d Regiment R. I. H. A.

George H. Abbott, Third Corporal. Promoted from Private June 4th. Sergeant in 9th Regiment R. I. V., (three months.)

George S. Banford, 4th Corporal. Discharged May 31st.

James E. O'Brien, Musician. Discharged May 8th. Private in 3d Regiment R. I. H. A.

ROLL OF THE REGIMENT.

James Marshall, Musician.
Albert H. Abbott.
Henry F. Abbott.
Wyllys A. Abbott.
William E. Adams. Sergeant in 5th Regiment R. I. V
Alanson A. Aldrich.
Thomas M. Aldrich.
George H. Allen. Sergeant in 9th Regiment R. I. V., (three months.)
Henry A. Arnold.
Ambrose L. Atwood. Sergeant in 9th Regiment R. I. V., three months.
Edwin H. Baker, Sergeant in 3d Regiment R. I. H. A.
Daniel W. Barnes. Wounded and taken prisoner at battle Bull Run, July 21st, 1861. Released, May, 1862.
William H. Blaisdell. Discharged May 31st.
Thomas Bolton. Died July 18th, 1861.
John Brown. Discharged June 14th. Sergeant in 39th Regiment New York volunteers.
Peleg E. Bryant. Appointed Sergeant in Carbineers, June 27th.
Samuel W Burbanks. Wounded in the battle of Bull Run. Sergeant in 5th Regiment R. I. V
George H. Burnham. Lieutenant in 9th Regiment R. I. V., three months.
William H. Burt.
Jasper Caler.
James H. Clarke. Sergeant 3d Regiment R. I. H. A.
John A. Clarke. Wounded and taken prisoner at the battle of Bull Run, July 21st, 1861. Appointed 2d Lieutenant, 2d Infantry, U. S. A., August 5th, 1861. Promoted to 1st Lieutenant, November 12th. Still a prisoner.
Henry C. Clarke.

APPENDIX D.

Willard Chaffee. Private in 3d Regiment R. I. H. A. Killed in the battle of James Island, June 16th, 1862.
Patrick Coleman. Sergeant in 3d Regiment R. I. H. A.
Thomas Cotton. Sergeant in 3d Regiment R. I. H. A.
George H. Cooke. Private in 3d Regiment R. I. H. A.
William H. H. Cowden. Private in 3d Regiment R. I. H. A.
Samuel B. T. Crandall. Corporal in 9th Regiment R. I. V. (3 months.)
George W. Davis.
William J. Davis.
George Dawley. Wounded in the battle of Bull Run, July 21st. Sergeant in 3d Regiment R. I. H. A.
Charles A. Dexter. Private in 3d Regiment R. I H. A. Deserted.
Cicero M. Dow. Private in 4th Regiment R. I. V
Joseph Dudley
Alpheus Eddy. Scout with Gen. Burnside.
Robert Elliott. Wounded in the battle of Bull Run, July 21st. Sergeant in 3d Regiment R. I. H. A.
Albert G. Evans. Lieutenant in 3d Regiment R. I. H. A.
Francis Evelyth. Wounded in the battle of Bull Run, July 21st. Private in 1st Regiment R. I. C.
George W. Field.
Charles W. Gardiner.
Jeremiah E. Gladden. Private in 1st Regiment R. I. L. A.
James Gregg. Sergeant in 5th Regiment R. I. V.
Franklin Gonsolve. Private in 7th Regiment R. I. V.
William Hardman, Jr.
Oliver Harrah.
Benjamin F. Hawkes. Discharged July 8th.
Amos M. Haskins. Wounded and taken prisoner at the battle of Bull Run, July 21st. Released May, 1861.
John C. Herbert. Sergeant in 4th Regiment R. I. V.
Horace B. Hilman. Detailed to War Department, May 2d.
Abraham H. Howarth.

ROLL OF THE REGIMENT. 187

Samuel Hyndman. Discharged July 3d. Private in 3d Regiment R. I. H. A.
Robert M. Irving. Wounded in the battle of Bull Run, July 21st, 1861
James M. Jaques. Sergeant in 3d Regiment R. I. H. A.
William H. Johnson.
Edward D. Kellogg. Discharged July 8th, 1861. Private in 2d Regiment R. I. V
Martin F. Kimball. Private in 3d Regiment R. I. H. A.
Thomas Lanphear. Private in 1st Regiment R. I. L. A.
Charles F. Lord. Private in 4th Regiment R. I. V
Alfred Luther. Private in 1st Regiment R. I. L. A.
James Lynch. Wounded in the battle of Bull Run, July 21st, 1861. Sergeant in 3d Regiment R. I. H. A.
Edward K. Mann. Private in 1st Regiment R. I. L. A.
James F. Maniman.
Edward Marr.
Edward C. Martin. Sergeant in 1st Regiment R. I. C.
James McCarty. Seaman in U. S. Navy.
James McEntee. Private in 1st Regiment R. I. L. A.
Charles McFarland. Private in 5th Regiment R. I. V
Benjamin F. Miller. Wounded in the battle of Bull Run.
Robert J. Mullen.
Michael Noon. Private in 10th Regiment R. I. V. (3 months.)
Elisha Peckham.
Alpheus Perry. Sergeant in 3d Regiment R. I. A.
Isaac H. Pinckney. Discharged May 31st.
Harris O. Potter. Private in 1st Regiment R. I. C.
Benjamin Powley.
Albert C. Randall.
Jeremiah Russell. Wounded in the battle of Bull Run, July 21st, 1861.
Daniel Sayles.
Charles C. Shattuck. Sergeant in 4th Regiment N. H. V.
William H. Shephard.

Hanson C. Smith.   Sergeant in 8th Regiment Maine volunteers.
Matthew Smith.   Private in 4th Regiment R. I. V
Stephen F. Smith.
Albert E. Sholes.   Sergeant in 4th Regiment R. I. V.
Daniel C. Snow.
Thomas Swan, Jr.
Lewis Warner.   Private in 3d Regiment R. I. H. A.
William Warner.
Orrin Wilson.
George A. Wooley.
James H. Zimmerman.

The nativities of this company were as follows:— Rhode Island, 45 ; Massachusetts, 10 ; Maine, 5 ; New Hampshire, 5 ; Vermont, 3 ; New York, 6 ; New Jersey, 2 ; Connecticut, 1 ; Michigan, 1 ; Pennsylvania, 1 ; England, 6 ; Ireland, 6 ; Scotland, 2 ; Germany, 1 ; Not returned, 14.   Total, 108.

Killed, none ; wounded, 11, of whom 3 were taken prisoners; died in service, 1.

Average age, 24½ years ; average height, 5 feet 7½ inches.

This company has furnished for the war, 1 Lieutenant Colonel ; 2 Captains ;* 1 Lieutenant ; 19 Sergeants ; 21 privates and 1 scout. To the army of the United States, 1 Lieutenant; and to the navy of the United States, 1 seaman. For three months' service, 1 Lieutenant Colonel ; 1 Captain ; 1 Lieutenant ; 3 Sergeants ; 1 Corporal, and 1 private.

COMPANY C.

William W. Brown, Captain.
Luther C. Warner, First Lieutenant.
Zephaniah Brown, Second Lieutenant.
Albert C. Eddy, Ensign.   Appointed Adjutant in 9th Regiment
    R. I. V. (3 mos.), May 26, 1862   Afterwards resigned.

---

* 1 Captain resigned.

ROLL OF THE REGIMENT. 189

Charles H. Dunham, First Sergeant. Appointed Captain in 9th Regiment R. I. V. (3 months), May 26th, 1862. Afterwards resigned.
John W. Gale, Second Sergeant.
James P. Fisher, Third Sergeant.
John A. Vaughan, Fourth Sergeant.
George E. Allen, First Corporal.
Henry K. Potter, Second Corporal.
Stephen A. Barker, Third Corporal.
Charles C. Ladd, Fourth Corporal.
Charles A. Allen. Sergeant in 10th Regiment R. I. V. (3 months.)
Christopher H. Alexander.
Edward F. Angell. Sergeant in 5th Regiment R. I. V.
William S. Angell.
Job Arnold. Captain in 5th Regiment R. I. V.
William R. Arnold.
Abraham Baker.
Byron C. Barrows.
Leonard S. Beals.
William H. Bean. Sergeant in 3d Regiment R. I. H. A.
Joseph L. Bennett, Jr. Lieutenant in 10th Regiment R. I. V (3 months.)
William B. Bennett.
John E. Bradford. Mustered May 29th. Lieutenant in 10th Regiment R. I. V. (3 months.)
J. M. Bradford. Mustered May 29th.
John M. Brannan.
Artemas Brown.
George H. Brown.
Henry A. Brown. Discharged May 31st.
Martin P. Buffum. Captain in 4th Regiment R. I. V
George E. Chase.
James E. Chase.
Edward F. Curtis. Lieutenant in 3d Regiment R. I. H. A.

APPENDIX D.

J. Madison Cutts, Jr. Discharged June 23d. Now Captain in 11th Regiment Infantry, U. S. A. Aide-de-Camp to Maj. Gen. Burnside.
Leander A. Davis. Sergeant in 5th Regiment R. I. V.
Henry A. DeWitt. Promoted to Engineer, May 31st.
James A. DeWolf. Assistant Paymaster, U. S. A.
Winthrop DeWolf. Mustered June 14th. Lieutenant in 10th Regiment R. I. V (3 months.)
Cornelius Draper.
George L. Draper. Sergeant in 1st Massachusetts Cavalry.
Amasa Eaton. Mustered June 8th.
Joseph A. Fowler.
Benjamin F. Goddard.
Francis W. Goddard. Promoted to Captain of Carbineers, June 27th.
Robert H. I. Goddard.
George O. Gorton. Promoted to Sergeant of Carbineers, June 27th. Lieutenant in 3d Regiment R. I. H. A.
William A. Grant.
Aaron S. Greene.
Arnold Green. Mustered May 29th.
Edward W. Greene.
William W. B. Greene. Lieutenant in 1st Regiment R. I. C. Resigned May, 1862.
Caleb B. Harrington. Mustered May 29th. Lieutenant in 10th Regiment R. I. V (3 months.)
William H. Helme.
Charles H. Hemmenway.
William W. Hoppin, Jr.
William C. Howland.
Pardon S. Jastram. Lieutenant in 1st Regiment R. I. L. A.
Moses B. Jenkins.
Orville B. Jones.
William D. Jones.
William H. Joyce.

ROLL OF THE REGIMENT. 191

Benjamin E. Kelly. Lieutenant in 1st Regiment R. I. L. A.
Oswald Ludwig.
Daniel H. Luther.
William T. Luther.
Charles S. Mathewson. Sergeant in 10th Regiment R. I. V. (3 months.)
Alexander H. Merritt.
Frank Molten. Mustered May 29th.
Albert W. Moore.
Henry C. Mowry. Discharged July 8th.
James T. Murray.
H. Frank Payton.
Henry Pearce. Lieutenant in Volunteer Battery, (3 months.)
James S. Peckham.
Charles H. Potter.
Isaac M. Potter. Lieutenant in 3d Regiment R. I. H. A.
Daniel S. Remington. Lieutenant in 5th Regiment R. I. V.
Orville M. Remington.
Henry Renches.
Charles W. Rhodes, Jr.
Robert Rhodes. Lieutenant in U. S. Navy.
Josiah W. Richardson. Taken prisoner at the battle of Bull Run, July 21st, and released August 12th, 1861.
Oscar Richardson. Mustered May 29th.
Lewis Richmond. Major,—Assistant Adjutant General of Major General Burnside's staff.
Bridgham C. Root.
Charles M. Smith.
T. Delap Smith. Mustered May 29th. Taken prisoner at the battle of Bull Run, July 21st. Since released.
William S. Smith. Captain in 10th Regiment R. I. V. (3 mos.)
Stephen W. Snow. Taken prisoner at the battle of Bull Run. Released May, 1862.
George P. Streeter. Discharged June 9th. Sergeant in 1st Regiment R. I. C.

James O. Swan.   Private in 10th Regiment R. I. V. (3 mos.)
John H. Sweet.
Alexander V. G. Taylor.
John G. Thurber, Jr.
William E. Thurston.
Clark P. Tillinghast.
Abel W. Tripp.   Discharged May 30th.
Charles D. Vaughan.
Abel Waite.   Corporal in 3d Regiment R. I. H. A.
John P. Walker.
Charles A. Warren.   Sergeant in 1st Regiment Massachusetts Volunteers.
James Warren, Jr.
Richard Waterman.   Lieutenant in 1st Reg't R. I. Cavalry.
Henry S. Weaver.
Theodore W. Webb.
Job H. Wells.
Edward N. Whittier.   Detailed for Hospital duty, June 23d. Lieutenant in 1st Maine Artillery Regiment.
Horatio G. Whittier, Jr.   Sergeant in a Massachusetts Regiment.
Charles C. Wightman.
Edward P. Wiley.
N. Bangs Williams.
Luther T. Winslow.
William C. Wood.   Captain in 4th Regiment R. I. V.
George F. Young.   Lieutenant in a New York artillery regiment.

The nativities of this company were as follows: Rhode Island, 77; Massachusetts, 8; New York, 5; Maine, 3; Connecticut, 5; New Hampshire, 1; District of Columbia, 1; England, 1; Ireland, 1. Not returned, 12. Total, officers and men, 114. Killed, none. Taken prisoners, 3.

Average age, 26. Oldest man, 58; youngest, 19.

Average height, 5 feet, 6 3-4 inches.

ROLL OF THE REGIMENT. 193

This company has furnished for the war, 1 Major of the Staff, 3 Captains of the Line, 11 Lieutenants,* 7 Sergeants, 1 Corporal; to the Army of the United States, 1 Captain, and 1 Assistant Paymaster; to the Navy of the United States, 1 Lieutenant; and to the service for three months, 2 Captains,† 1 Adjutant,† 5 Lieutenants, 2 Sergeants, and 1 Private.

COMPANY D

Nathaniel W. Brown, Captain. Appointed Colonel of 3d Regiment R. I. H. A., September 18, 1861. Res'd July, '62.

Sylvester R. Knight, 1st Lieutenant. Taken prisoner at Centreville, July 22d. Released, and returned to Providence, January 25th, 1862.

Henry A. Prescott, 2d Lieutenant. Killed at the battle of Bull Run, while bravely leading his men.

Charles R. Dennis, Ensign.

J. Harry Welch, First Sergeant.

A. Richmond Rawson, 2d Sergeant. Lieutenant in 3d Regiment R. I. H. A.

John M. Barker, Third Sergeant. Lieutenant in 3d Regiment R. I. H. A.

James L. Richardson, Fourth Sergeant. Adjutant of 3d Regiment R. I. H. A.

William E. Cutting, First Corporal.

George H. Wescott, Second Corporal. Discharged June 22d.

Samuel Foster, 2d., Third Corporal. Missing at the battle of Bull Run, and not heard from.

Franklin E. Chase, Fourth Corporal. Adjutant of 4th Regiment R. I. V

Greis Leopold, Musician.

Edward Aborn. Mustered May 30th. Private in 10th Regiment R. I. V., (three months.)

---

*1 Lieutenant resigned; †1 Captain and 1 Adjutant resigned.

APPENDIX D.

Charles T. Almy.
William H. Ambrose.
Theodore Andrews.
John Rice Arnold. Died at Providence, July 30th.
John E. Austin.
Charles E. Bailey. Mustered May 30th.
Frederic S. Batcheller.
James L. Bennett.
Joel B. Blaisdell.
Charles H. Bliss.
Charles H. Bogman. Wounded at the battle of Bull Run, July 21st. Sergeant in 1st Regiment R. I. L. A.
Loammi Boutwell.
William P. Bradford.
George W. Brockett. Lieutenant in 5th Regiment Connecticut Volunteers.
Levi B. Brown. Discharged June 4th.
Albert W Bullock. Wounded at the battle of Bull Run, July 21st, 1861.
John E. Burroughs. Sergeant in 3d Regiment R. I. H. A.
William H. H. Butts.
George Carpenter. Wounded at the battle of Bull Run, July 21, 1861. Quartermaster of 3d Regiment R. I. H. A
John F. Caulkins.
William Chace.
Lafayette Chapman.
George A. Church.
David B. Churchill. Lieutenant in 3d Regiment R. I. H. A.
Samuel G. Colwell.
Jesse Comstock. Wounded, taken prisoner at the battle of Bull Run, and died at Sudley, July 31st, 1861.
Thomas Craig. Private in volunteer battery, (three months.)
Horace H. Darling.
Moses O. Darling. Lieutenant in 10th Regiment R. I. V., (three months.)

ROLL OF THE REGIMENT. 195

William B. Deblois.
Charles B. Delanah. Sergeant in 1st Regiment R. I. C.
Richard H. Demming. Appointed Sergeant Major in 1st Regiment R. I. L. A. Afterwards resigned.
William B. Dennis. Appointed Lieutenant in 1st Regiment R. I. Cavalry. Afterwards resigned.
William H. DeWolf. Master's mate U. S. N.
John Antoine Duvillard. Mustered May 30th. Lieutenant in 12th Regiment of Infantry, U. S. A., Oct. 24, 1861.
Christopher J. Dodge, Jr. Mustered May 30th.
Charles H. Fisher.
George W. Flagg, mortally wounded, taken prisoner at the battle of Bull Run, and died at Gordonsville, Aug. 3, 1861.
Munroe H. Gladding. Quartermaster of 5th Regiment R. I. V
Charles E. Glines.
William H. Goodhue.
George E. Goulding.
Philo P. Hawkes.
Richard B. Hawkins.
Charles C. Henry.
Thomas W D. Horton.
William M. Houghton. Master's Mate U. S. N.
Albert E. Hudson.
James S. Hudson.
Charles O. Jackson. Saddler in 1st Regiment R. I. L. A.
Leland D. Jenckes. Wounded and taken prisoner at the battle of Bull Run, July 21, 1861. Released May, 1862.
Henry A. Jewett.
Albert P. Johonnot. Promoted to be Corporal, June 23d.
Henry C. Johnson. Mustered May 30th.
Sanford A. Kingsley. Mustered May 30th.
George W Kinney.
William A. Knight. Mustered May 30th.
Frank H. Knowles.

Charles Lapham.
Edwin A. Leavens.
Edwin Lowe. Discharged June 4th.
Walter B. Manton. Promoted to Lieutenant of Carbineers, June 27th. Lieut. in 3d Regiment R. I. H. A.
Henry W. Mason. Sergeant in 3d Regiment R. I. H. A.
Gilbert D. McCormick. Scout with Major General Burnside's Expedition. Since returned.
George Metcalf. Mustered May 30th. Lieutenant in 3d Regment R. I. H. A.
Henry H. Metcalf. Sergeant in 1st Regiment R. I. L. A.
Robert Nevins. Lieutenant in 3d Regiment R. I. H. A.
Edward A. Osborn.
George H. Paddock.
Edward S. Parker. Private in 10th Regiment R. I. V. (three months.)
William B. Pearce.
Charles B. Pennel.
Albert B. Penno. Wounded and taken prisoner at the battle of Bull Run, and died at Richmond, Aug. 4.
Ebenezer W. Percival.
Joseph W. Pratt. Steward of U. S. Hospital, Providence.
Charles S. Presby.
William W. Prouty. Quartermaster's Sergeant in 5th Regiment R. I. V.
William W Rathbun. Appointed Sutler in 4th Regiment R. I. V.; afterwards returned home.
George H. Rhodes. Lieutenant in 1st Regiment R. I. C.
William H. Rhodes.
Reuben C. Ruggles. Mustered May 30th.
Stephen Russell.
Frederick M. Sackett. Lieut. in 1st Regiment R. I. L. A.
Isaac H. Saunders. Mustered May 30th.
Albert T. Shurtleff. Wounded and taken prisoner at the battle of Bull Run July 21st. Released.

ROLL OF THE REGIMENT. 197

Noyes J. Smith. Discharged June 4th.
George A. Spink. Lieutenant in 10th Regiment R. I. V., (three months).
Levi Starbuck.
Lorenz Steinbring.
Moses Sweeten.
Peleg G. Tallman.
Charles H. Thayer. Detailed to Hospital, June 23d. Lieutenant in 1st Regiment R. I. C.
Benjamin F. Thomas.
Andrew C. Thompson.
Edward K. Thompson.
Henry H. Thornton.
Lewis H. Trescott. Wounded at the battle of Bull Run July 21st.
Henry W. Tucker.
Eben W Waterhouse. Lieutenant in 1st Regiment R. I. H. A.
Charles S. Whipple.
Henry W Whitman. Discharged, June 22d.
Nicholas B. Young.
Thomas Young. Detailed to Hospital duty July 4th. Quartermaster of N. Y. Artillery Regiment.

The nativities of this company were as follows: Rhode Island, 53; Massachusetts, 25; New York, 9; Connecticut, 6; Vermont, 2; Maine, 2; New Hampshire, 2; Germany, 2; Scotland, 1; not returned, 15. Total, officers and men, 117.

Killed, 1 officer; taken prisoner, 1 officer; mortally wounded and taken prisoner, 3; wounded and taken prisoner, 2; wounded, 4; missing, 1; died in service, 1.

Average age, 26 3-4 years. Oldest man, 42; youngest, 18. Average height, 5 feet, 7 1-2 inches.

This company has furnished for the war, 1 Colonel, 11 Lieutenants, 2 Adjutants, 3 Quartermasters, 1 Sergeant Major, 6 Sergeants, 1 Sutler, 1 Steward, 1 Scout, 1 Saddler; to the army of the United States, 1 Lieutenant; to the navy of the United

17*

States, 2 Master's Mates; and to the service for three months, 2 Lieutenants and 3 Privates. One Colonel, one Lieutenant, 1 Sergeant Major, 1 Sutler, and 1 Scout have belonged to the service for three years, but resigned, after having gone into the field.

COMPANY E.

Stephen R. Bucklin, Captain. Lieut. Colonel of 3d Regiment R. I. H. A.
William R. Walker, First Lieutenant. Clerk in Department of Interior.
Lucien B. Stone, Second Lieutenant. Resigned, June 4th.
Robert McCloy, Second Lieutenant. Promoted from 1st Sergeant June 5th. Captain in 7th Regiment R. I. V
Levi Tower, Ensign. Resigned June 1st, and appointed Captain in 2d Regiment R. I. V Killed at battle of Bull Run, July 21, 1861.
Robert McCloy, First Sergeant. Promoted to be 2d Lieutenant, June 5th.
Albert W. Tompkins, Second Sergeant. Promoted to be 1st Sergeant June 5th. Lieutenant in 9th Regiment R. I. V (three months.)
Henry C. Brown, Third Sergeant. Adjutant of 9th Regiment R. I. V (three months.)
Augustus W. Colwell, Fourth Sergeant. Lieut. in 3d Regiment R. I. H. A.
Oliver H. Perry, First Corporal. Promoted to be Sergeant, June 5th. Sergeant in 9th Regiment R. I. V. (three months.)
William Sang, Second Corporal. Discharged May 31.
Edward Taft, Third Corporal.
William Eason, Fourth Corporal. Landsman, U. S. N.
George L. Keech, Musician. Private in 3d Reg't R. I. H. A.

ROLL OF THE REGIMENT. 199

Frederic Schneider, Musician. Corporal in 9th Regiment R. I. V. (three months.)
John Aigan. Lieutenant in 3d Regiment R. I. H. A.
John R. Anderson. Sergeant in 7th Regiment R. I. V.
Benjamin O. Arnold.
Cyrus V. Bacon.
Stephen Ballou. Private in 9th Regiment R. I. V., (3 mos.)
Francisco Ballou.
Nelson Ballou.
William Beatty.
Charles Bliss. Hospital steward in 1st Regiment R. I. C.
Julius J. Bosworth.
James A. Brown. Private in 9th Regiment R. I. V. (3 mos.)
Henry A. Burchard.
Henry L. Carter.
Samuel Cash.
William H. Chace. Discharged July 2d. Corporal in 7th Regiment R. I. V.
William Clark.
William Coupe. Wounded in battle of Bull Run. Lieut. in 1st Regiment Mass. Cav.
John E. Cowden.
Charles C. Crocker. Corporal in 9th Regiment R. I. V., (three months.)
Frederic Dexter. Died at Cumberland, August 10, 1861.
George A. Earle. Sergeant in 1st Regiment R. I. C.
Thomas A. Earle. Sergeant in 1st Regiment R. I. C.
Joseph P. Farnsworth. Sergeant in 5th Regiment R. I. V.
George J. Fairbrother.
Robert Fessenden. Sergeant Major in 9th Regiment R. I. V., (three months.)
James A. Gardner.
Clarence T. Gardner. Sergeant in 3d Regiment R. I. H. A.
Cyrus B. Hathaway. Lieutenant in 7th Regiment R. I. V.
William Heipe. Sergeant in 3d Regiment R. I. H. A.

APPENDIX D.

Nathaniel M. Ingalls. Private in 2d Regiment R. I. V.
William A. Jackson. Private in 1st Regiment Mass. Cav.
Jabez E. Jenks. Wounded in battle of Bull Run, July 21.
Charles H. Johnson. Lieutenant in 4th Regiment R. I. V
Daniel L. Johnson. Corporal in 9th Regiment R. I. V., (three months.)
Jirey Kenney, Jr. Sergeant in 7th Regiment R. I. V.
Royal II. Lee. Sergeant Major in 1st Regiment R. I. L. A.
Augustus Little.
Samuel H. Luther.
George F. Lyon.
Pardon Mason. Promoted to Corporal, June 5th. Capt, in 3d Regiment R. I. II. A.
George Macomber.
George A. Mason. Promoted to Corporal, June 5th.
John McKelvey. Wounded in battle of Bull Run, July 21, 1861. Enlisted in 3d Reg't R. I. H. A., and disabled. Afterwards Corporal in 7th Regiment R. I. V.
Frank Merry. Discharged, June 9th.
Ira E. Miller.
Augustus Mowry.
George D. Morris. Corporal in 9th Regiment R. I. V., (three months.)
Robert Murray. Discharged, June 26th.
George W Newell. Private in 9th Regiment R. I. V., (three months.)
Isaac Nickerson, Jr.
Dean Nickerson, Jr.
Thomas O. Nickerson. Corporal in 3d Regiment R. I. H. A.
Lebbeus Northup. Corporal in 3d Regiment R. I. H. A.
William C. Olney. Sergeant in 4th Regiment R. I. V
Edwin R. Paine.
Walter F. Padelford.
James T. Pearce. Private in 3d Regiment R. I. II. A.
David Perrin. Wounded in battle of Bull Run, July 21.

ROLL OF THE REGIMENT.

William Phillips. Sergeant in 3d Regiment R. I. H. A.
John M. Pollard.
Henry Pollard.
Thomas Rankin.
John Ramsbottom. Sergeant in 7th Regiment R. I. V
Andrew J. Radloff.
Benjamin C. Rhodes. Discharged, July 2.
Joseph A. Rhodes. Sergeant in 1st Regiment R. I. C.
Randall H. Rice. Lieut. in 11th Regiment Conn. Vol.
Arnold Salisbury. Sergeant in 7th Regiment R. I. V.
George H. Salisbury. Private in 4th Regiment R. I. V.
George M. Salisbury. Private in 4th Regiment R. I. V.
George Schneider. Corporal in 9th Reg't R. I. V (3 mos.)
David Sherman. Sergeant in 3d Regiment R. I. H. A.
Francis Slaiger. Private in 1st Regiment R. I. L. A.
Joseph Slaiger. Sergeant in 3d Regiment R. I. H. A.
Lyman F. Slocum.
Charles Smith. Sergeant in 5th Regiment R. I. V.
James Munroe Smith. Private in 7th Regiment R. I. V.
Peter Stephens. Corporal in 4th Regiment R. I. V.
John E. Stearns. Sergeant in 1st Regiment R. I. L. A.
Charles Taft. Sergeant in 5th Regiment R. I. V.
Joseph Taylor. Private 3d Reg't R. I. H. A. Mustered, June 6.
Kimball Tilton. Wounded, July 21, 1861, in battle of Bull Run.
   Sergeant in a N. H. regiment.
Ferdinand Tisdale. Lieutenant in 3d Regiment R. I. H. A.
Samuel E. Tracy. Master's Mate, U. S. N.
John Turner.
James Watson.
Thomas C. Webb.
Walter Wheeler, Jr. Sergeant in 3d Regiment R. I. H. A.
Arlon M. Whipple.
Henry C. Wickson.
James N. Woodward.

APPENDIX D.

The nativities of this company were as follows:—Rhode Island, 45; Massachusetts, 32; Connecticut, 4; Maine, 3; New York, 3; New Hampshire, 1; England, 4; Bavaria, 2; Ireland, 2; Germany, 2; Wirtemberg, 2; Prussia, 1; Scotland, 1; not returned, 3. Total, Officers and men, 105.

Wounded, 5.

Average age, 25 years; oldest man, 47; youngest, 18. Average height, 5 feet 8 inches.

This company has furnished for the war, 1 Lieut. Colonel; 3 Captains;* 7 Lieutenants; 1 Sergeant Major; 19 Sergeants; 5 Corporals; 1 Hospital steward and 9 privates; to the navy of the United States, 1 Master's mate and 1 landsman; and to the service for three months, 1 Adjutant; 1 Lieutenant; 1 Sergeant Major; 1 Sergeant; 5 Corporals and 3 privates.

COMPANY F

George W Tew, Captain. Lieut. Colonel 4th Reg't R. I. V.
William A. Stedman. First Lieutenant.
Benjamin L. Slocum, Second Lieutenant. Captain in 10th Regiment R. I. V (three months.)
James H. Chappell, Ensign.
Augustus P. Sherman, First Sergeant.
Thomas S. Burdick, Second Sergeant.
John S. Coggeshall, Third Sergeant.
Edward S. Hammond, Fourth Sergeant.
John D. Washburn, First Corporal.
Benedict F. Smith, Second Corporal.
Ray B. Sayer, Third Corporal.
Henry L. Nicolai, Fourth Corporal. Sergeant in 1st Regiment R. I. C.
Charles B. Barlow, Musician. Master's mate U. S. N. Promoted to Acting Master, July, 1862.

---

* 1 Captain killed.

Albert N. Burdick, Musician. Wounded at battle of Bull Run, July 21. Lieut. in 4th Regiment R. I. V Resigned July, 1862.
John A. Abbott. Private in 3d Regiment R. I. H. A. Discharged May 21.
George C. Almy.
John H. Bachelor.
Christopher E. Barker.
Charles Barker, Jr.
Andrew P. Bashford. Taken prisoner at Bull Run, July 21. Escaped and retaken twice. Released December, 1861. Now Master's mate, U. S. N.
William Booth.
Daniel A. Boss. Private in 4th Regiment R. I. V. Died at Beaufort, N. C., June, 1862.
Jeremiah Brown. Captain in 4th Regiment R. I. V
Adelbert P. Bryant.
Thomas S. Brownell.
Henry Bull, Jr.
Benjamin D. Carlile.
Robert Carlile, Jr.
Allen Caswell. Wounded at battle of Bull Run, July 21.
Charles H. Clarke.
Edward F. Clarke.
Frederic A. Clarke.
Gustavus A. Clarke.
Joshua P. Clarke. Sergeant in 4th Regiment R. I. V Promoted to Lieutenant, July, 1862.
David M. Coggeshall, Jr.
Lawton Coggeshall. Mustered May 29. Master's mate U. S. N.
Robert D. Coggeshall.
Robert M. Crane.
Perry B. Dawley. Watchman at the Naval School, Newport.
Benjamin F. Davis.
William P. Denman. Corporal in 4th Regiment R. I. V.

Lance De Jongh. Private in 10th Regiment R. I. V. (3 mos.)
Silas D. Deblois.
Stephen Deblois.
William H. Durfee, Jr. Discharged July 12. Private in 5th Regiment R. I. V.
John F. Easton.
Benjamin Easton, Jr.
Henry F. Easton. Wounded at battle of Bull Run, July 21, 1861.
William J. Eldridge.
Edmund W. Fales. Sergeant in 10th Reg't R. I. V. (3 mos.)
John Fludder. Private in 10th Regiment R. I. V (3 mos.)
Augustus French. Watchman at the Naval School, Newport.
Joseph J. Gould. Captain in 1st Regiment R. I. C.
Thomas Harrington, Jr. Killed at battle of Bull Run, July 21.
Rowland R. Hazard.
William Hamilton.
Samuel Hilton. Wounded at battle of Bull Run, July 21. Private in 4th Regiment R. I. V.
Benjamin C. Hubbard.
George A. Hudson. Private in 4th Regiment R. I. V.
Harris F. Keables.
William Keating. Private in 1st Regiment R. I. C.
Edwin A. Kelly. Private in 1st Regiment R. I. C.
T. Wheaton King. Wounded and taken prisoner at battle of Bull Run, July 21. Died at Philadelphia, January 28, 1862.
William H. King. Mustered May 29. Lieutenant in 10th Regiment R. I. V (3 months.)
Israel F. Lake, Jr. Private in 4th Regiment R. I. V.
Thomas O. Lake. Private in 4th Regiment R. I. V.
Henry B. Landers. Lieutenant in 5th Regiment R. I. V,
John B. Landers. Wounded at battle of Bull Run, July 21. Private in 10th Regiment R. I. V. (3 months.)
Overton G. Langley.

Charles E. Lawton.
George P. Lawton. Discharged July 2.
Thomas H. Lawton. Discharged May 21.
David Little. Discharged May 31.
Charles L. Littlefield.
John B. Mason.
James Markham. Private in 4th Regiment R. I. V.
Daniel A. McCann.
William M. Minkler. Private in 10th Reg't R. I. V (3 mos.)
Walden H. Nason.
Michael A. Nolan.
George H. Palmer.
Frederic J. Peabody. Discharged May 31. Private in 4th Regiment R. I. V
Edwin H. Peabody. Private in 4th Regiment R. I. V
John P. Peckham. Killed in the battle of Bull Run, July 21, 1861.
Peyton H. Randolph. Captain's clerk, U. S. Navy.
John Rogers. Wounded in the battle of Bull Run, July 21, 1861. Capt. in 1st Regiment R. I. C.
Benjamin H. Rogers. Sergeant in 1st Regiment R. I. L. A.
John H. Robinson.
John F. Scott. Sergeant in 1st Regiment R. I. C.
Thomas Scott. Hospital duty, May 2, 1861.
Thomas Sharp.
Bartlett L. Simmons. Taken prisoner at Bull Run, July 21, 1861. Released, May, 1862.
John B. F. Smith. Master's mate, U. S. N.
George B. Smith.
Charles Southwick.
John Stark. Private in a New York regiment.
George W. Taber. Private in 10th Reg't R. I. V (3 mos.)
Edward Terrell.
William H. Thayer.
William Towle.

Arthur B. Tuel.
James P. Vose. Lieutenant in 1st Regiment R. I. C.
William H. Waldron. Discharged May 31.
George S. Ward. Discharged July 12.
Charles S. Weaver.
George R. White. Private in 4th Regiment R. I. V
Edward Wilson. Discharged July 12.
William Young.

The nativities of this company were as follows:— Rhode Island, 73; Massachusetts, 6; Maine, 2; New York, 2; Pennsylvania, 1; Maryland, 1; Illinois, 1; Vermont, 1; England, 4; Ireland, 2; Scotland, 2; Germany, 1; Not returned, 12. Total, officers and men, 108.

Killed, 2; wounded, taken prisoner, and died on his way home, 1; wounded 6; taken prisoner, 2.

Average age, 23 3-4 years. Oldest man, 44; youngest, 18. Average height, 5 feet 7 inches.

This company has furnished for the war, 1 Lieutenant Colonel; 3 Captains; 4 Lieutenants;* 3 Sergeants; 1 Corporal and 14 privates;† to the navy of the United States, 1 acting Master; 3 Master's Mates; and 1 Captain's Clerk; to the Naval School, 2 Watchmen; and to the service, for three months, 1 Captain; 1 Lieutenant; 1 Sergeant; and 4 privates.

COMPANY G

David A. Peloubet went in command of this company as far as Annapolis, and returned thence to Providence. He is now in command of a company in Colonel John Cochrane's regiment of New York Chasseurs.

John T. Pitman, Captain. Mustered May 6. Lieut. Col. in 9th Regiment R. I. V. (3 months.) Promoted to Colonel, June, 1862.

---

* 1 Lieutenant resigned.   † 1 Private deceased.

ROLL OF THE REGIMENT. 207

Albert G. Bates, First Lieutenant.
Edward Luther, Second Lieutenant.
John L. Bushee, Ensign. In commissary department of a Wisconsin regiment.
George B. Lapham, First Sergeant. Detailed to Ordnance Department, May 21st.
Charles G. Strahan, First Sergeant. Promoted from Private, May 21st. Capt. in 3d Regiment R. I. H. A.
Charles Becherer, Second Sergeant. Color Sergeant. Wounded in the battle of Bull Run, July 21st, 1861.
James W. Henry, Third Sergeant. Sergeant Major in 1st Regiment R. I. C.
Latham T Babcock, Fourth Sergeant. Sergeant in 3d Regiment R. I. H. A.
Charles W. Tibbitts, First Corporal. Laborer in Navy Yard, Washington, D. C.
James Seamans, Second Corporal. Taken prisoner in the battle of Bull Run, July 21, 1861. Released, May, 1862.
John E. Bennett. Third Corporal. Sergeant in 1st Regiment R. I. C.
Charles G. A. Peterson, Fourth Corporal. Sergeant in 1st Regiment R. I. C. Promoted to Lieut. June 6, 1862.
Horace F. Allen. Private in 7th Squadron R. I. C., (three months.)
Augustus Ball.
Henry Borden.
John S. Brown. Corporal in 1st Regiment R. I. C.
Samuel Brown. Private in 1st Regiment R. I. C.
Cornelius Brassline. Corporal in 1st Regiment R. I. C.
Gardiner Bryant. Wounded in the battle of Bull Run, July 21st, 1861. Private in 7th Squadron R. I. C. (three months.)
Gustavus B. Burlingame. Sergeant in 10th Regiment R. I. V., (three months.)
James H. Burbank. Private in 4th Regiment R. I. V.

Hezekiah O. Bucklin.
James C. Burke. Private in 1st Regiment R. I. C.
Raymond W Cahoon. Sergeant in 10th Regiment R. I. V.,
    (three months).
Edward E. Carpenter.
William Cassada. Private in 1st Regiment R. I. C.
James Clark.
Thomas C. Clark. Sergeant in 1st Regiment R. I. C.
Thomas Costello.
William R. Cook.
Ozias J. Danforth. Private in 1st Regiment R. I. L. A.
Raphael E. Dexter, Sergeant in 1st Regiment R. I. C.
Paul Downs. Taken prisoner in the battle of Bull Run, July
    21. Died, at Richmond, August 1, 1861.
Stephen A. Farguison.
Lewis Florsheim.
James C. Forsyth. Discharged June 13th.
Page F. Grover.
Charles Grosse. Private in 4th Regiment R. I. V
Charles Harkens. Private in 4th Regiment R. I. V
Robert Hausensteine.
Lewis T. Hall. Promoted to Sergeant in Carbineers June 27th.
Robert Haydon. Corporal in 4th Regiment R. I. V.
Alvinzi Healy.
James E. Hill.
William Hoffman.
William E. Hooper. Private in 3d Regiment R. I. II. A.
William Hounam. Wounded and taken prisoner in the battle
    of Bull Run, July 21, 1861. Released, May, 1862.
Daniel Holmes. Private in 4th Regiment R. I. V.
Edward Holmes. Wounded and taken prisoner in the battle
    of Bull Run, July 21, 1861. Released, May, 1862.
Thomas H. Holmes.
William F. Holmes. Sergeant in 1st Regiment R. I. C.
James Hughes.

ROLL OF THE REGIMENT.

Michael Hughes. Discharged May 12th.
George W. Hull. Discharged June 1st.
Dennis Hynes. Sergeant in 3d Regiment R. I. H. A.
Hugh Johnson. Seaman in U. S. N. Discharged, May, 1862.
James B. Johnson. Private in 1st Regiment R. I. C.
David G. Jones.
Owen L Leach. Sergeant in 1st Regiment R. I. C.
Jabez Lord.
Walter H. Luther. Sergeant in 5th Regiment R. I. V.
Patrick Maddison.
John J. Mangold.
Thomas Martin. Discharged May 12th.
William D. McCoy.
James C. McAdams. Discharged June 13th.
Arthur J. McAllen.
Owen McElroy. Private in 1st Regiment R. I. L. A.
George McGunnigle. Private in 1st Regiment R. I. L. A.
James McGunnigle. Private in 1st Regiment R. I. L. A..
Thomas McMahon. Sergeant in 4th Regiment R. I. V.
James Morning. Private in 10th Regiment R. I. V. (3 mos.)
James Munroe.
John Marshall.
Edward E. Nichols. Discharged June 1st.
William M. Nottage. Corporal in 4th Regiment R. I. V.
William H. Packard. Wounded in the battle of Bull Run, July 21st, 1861.
Harry D. Perkins. Taken prisoner in the battle of Bull Run, July 21, 1861. Sergeant in 10th Regiment R. I. V. (three months.)
Stephen H. Pickering. Corporal in 1st Regiment R. I. C.
John Pitman, Jr. Private in 10th Regiment R. I. V (3 mos.)
James Redin.
Joseph Pollard. Wounded and taken prisoner in the battle of Bull Run, July 21st. Released, May, 1862.
Christopher C. Rhodes.

Charles F. Rhodes. Private in 4th Regiment R. I. V.
William E. Rhodes. Discharged June 1st. Seaman in U. S. N.
John H. Richards.
John Rothwell. Private in 1st Regiment R. I. C.
Herman Schocher. Killed in the battle of Bull Run, July 21st.
Robert Seiler. In Band of 3d Regiment R. I. H. A.
David Shaw. Private in 1st Regiment R. I. L. A.
William Shaw.
Silas Spink.
Henry P. Stafford. Wounded and taken prisoner in the battle of Bull Run, July 21, 1861. Released, May, 1862.
Charles Stuart. Private in 3d Regiment R. I. H. A.
Henry A. Sunderland. Private in 1st Regiment R. I. L. A.
Thomas H. Sweetland. Sergeant in 5th Regiment R. I. V.
John W. Taylor. Discharged May 14th. Private in 9th Regiment R I. V., (3 months.)
William F. Tanzey. Sergeant in 5th Regiment R. I. V.
Henry E. Testen. Private in 1st Regiment R. I. L. A. Killed in the battle of James' Mill, June 27, 1862.
James A. Thornton. Sergeant in 1st Regiment R. I. C.
Frederic Thoene.
George Trautz. Private in 4th Regiment R. I. V.
Thomas J. Ward.
Edward Wilkins.
Justus K. Watson.
Franklin E. Wilmarth. Corporal in 5th Regiment R. I. V
George W. Young.
August Zimmer.

Commissary Department.

Charles Munroe.
Cyrus Peabody.
Charles J. Place. Private 9th Regiment R. I. V. (3 mos.)
Charles H. Rounds. Sergeant in 9th Reg't R. I. V. (3 mos.)

NOTE.—Samuel S. Dexter was mustered into service with this company, but was detailed to become servant to Major

Slocum, and accompanied that officer when he was promoted to the command of the 2d Regiment R. I. V.

The nativities of this company were as follows: Rhode Island, 48; Massachusetts, 11; New York, 7; New Jersey, 2; New Hampshire, 1; Maine, 1; Connecticut, 1; Germany, 8; Ireland, 8; England, 8; Nova Scotia, 2; Prussia, 2; Scotland, 2; Holland, 1; Switzerland, 1. Not returned, 10. Total, officers and men, 113. Killed, 1; mortally wounded and taken prisoner, 1; wounded, 3; wounded and taken prisoner, 4; taken prisoner, 2.

Average age, 25¾ years. Oldest man, 48; youngest, 18.

Average height, 5 feet, 6¾ inches.

This company has furnished for the war, 1 Captain; 1 Lieutenant; 1 Sergeant Major; 12 Sergeants; 6 Corporals; 19 privates;* 1 clerk in commissary department; to a regimental band, 1 private; to the navy of the United States, 2 seamen,† and 1 laborer in Navy yard; and to the service for three months, 1 Colonel; 3 Sergeants, and 8 privates.

COMPANY H.

Charles W. H. Day, Captain. Captain in 3d Reg't R. I. H. A.
Joseph Brooks, Jr., First Lieutenant.
Earl C. Harris, Second Lieutenant.
Asa A. Ellis, Ensign. Lieutenant in 3d Regiment R. I. H. A.
John A. Irving, First Sergeant.
Calvin G. Cahoone, 2d, Second Sergeant. Lieutenant in 4th
    Regiment R. I. V
Michael Costello, Third Sergeant.
Joseph Burgess, 2d, Fourth Sergeant. Sergeant in 3d Regiment R. I. H. A.

---

*1 Private killed.   †1 Seaman discharged.

APPENDIX D.

Daniel L. Arnold, First Corporal. Promoted from Private. July 23. Sergeant in 3d Regiment R. I. H. A. Mortally wounded in the battle of James Island, June 16, and died June 24, 1862.

George L. Kibby, Second Corporal. Discharged July 8th. Corporal in 4th Regiment R. I. V.

John R. Arnold, Second Corporal. Promoted from Private, July 8th. Sergeant in 1st Regiment R. I. C.

Joseph Howcroft, Third Corporal. Accidentally wounded at Williamsport, June 15th, and discharged July 12th, 1861. Sergeant in 3d Regiment R. I. H. A.

George H. Read, Fourth Corporal.

William A. Abbott, Musician. Sergeant in 1st Reg't R. I. C.

Frank B. Young, Musician.

John C. Ash.

John G. Becker.

Jeremiah Bennett. Discharged May 31st. Private in 1st Regiment R. I. L. A.

James A. Bowen. Discharged May 9th. Private in 3d Regiment R. I. H. A.

Edward Bidmead.

Constantine Bischoff. Sergeant in 5th Regiment R. I. V.

John E. Bowen.

Robert S. Brownell. Sergeant in 5th Regiment R. I. V

Richard A. Bright.

Charles Brotherton.

Philip M. Bullock.

Davis C Burke.

David W. Carrington. Private in 3d Regiment R. I. H. A.

John F. Carpenter. Private in 3d Regiment R. I. H. A.

Samuel J. Chace.

Alexander Charnley. Discharged May 31st.

Henry Cook. Private in 1st Regiment R. I. C.

Salvica Cook. Private in 1st Regiment R. I. L. A.

Patrick Curley. Private in 1st Regiment R. I. L. A.

ROLL OF THE REGIMENT. 213

Joseph Dean. Discharged May 9th. Sergeant in a N. Y. Artillery regiment.
Newton Dow.
Thomas A. Dolan. Lieutenant in a New York Artillery Reg't.
James Dougherty. Killed in the battle of Bull Run, July 21st.
William H. Earle. Discharged July 8th.
John Falvey. Taken prisoner at Centreville, July 22d, and died July 28th, 1861.
John A. Farrell. Private in 10th Reg't R. I. V (3 mos.)
Lawrence Farrell. Corporal in 3d Regiment R. I. H. A.
George A. Gardiner. Private in 2d Regiment R. I. V
Gustavus B. Gardiner. Sergeant in 4th Regiment R. I. V.
Thomas L. Greene. Corporal in 4th Regiment R. I. V.
William E. Greene.
Arthur Hargrave. Private in 1st Regiment R. I. L. A.
John C. Harris.
George Harker. Private in 3d Regiment R. I. H. A.
Augustus Hable.
James C. Haskins. Sergeant in 3d Regiment R. I. H. A.
John Hawkes.
Luke Healy. Private in 4th Regiment R. I. V.
Owen Heganey. Sergeant in 3d Regiment R. I. H. A.
Lewis A. Holmes.
Alfred I. Hopkins. Corporal in 3d Regiment R. I. H. A.
John Hughes. Sergeant in 3d Regiment R. I. H. A.
James Huyberts. Corporal in 4th Regiment R. I. V.
Lewis Inglehart.
James Kelley. Private in 3d Regiment R. I. H. A.
Michael Kelley. Private in 5th Regiment R. I. V
William H. Kelley. Private in 4th Regiment R. I. H. A.
George W Lake. Discharged July 8th. Private in 3d Regiment R. I. H. A.
Joseph Lane.
Charles S. Lee. Corporal in 1st Regiment R. I. C.
Joseph F. Makee. Sergeant in a N. Y. Artillery regiment.

Hugh Manes.
John H. Mangold.
William H. Martin. Sergeant in 4th Regiment R. I. V
Peter A. Marsh.
John F. May. Sergeant in 1st Regiment R. I. C.
Albert Moessner. Corporal in 3d Regiment R. I. H. A.
Luke C. Moore. Seaman in U. S. navy.
Tappan W. Morrill.
Joseph Moshier. Private in 1st Regiment R. I. C.
John McCanna. Private in 2d Regiment R. I. V
Bernard McDonough. Private in 2d Regiment R. I. V
Michael McElroy. Private in 1st Regiment R. I. L. A.
James McQuestion.
George H. Nickerson. Private in 1st Regiment R. I. L. A.
Horace M. Nickerson. Private in 4th Regiment R. I. V.
Charles Norton.
George Nottage. Corporal in 4th Regiment R. I. V.
Royal J. Packard. Private in 3d Regiment R. I. H. A.
George Parker.
John A. Potter.
Michael Regan. Discharged July 8th. Seaman in U. S. N.
George M. Rice. Corporal in New York Chasseurs.
Henry Reynolds.
James E. Slocum. Wounded in battle of Bull Run, July 21st.
George Springer. Corporal in 4th Regiment R. I. V.
Edward L. Surgens. Wounded in the battle of Bull Run, July 21st.
Henry Thayer. Corporal in 3d Regiment R. I. H. A.
Nicholas W Thornton.
John H. Thurber. Private in 4th Regiment R. I. V
Frederic Trask.
William H. Trim. Discharged July 8th. Private in 1st Regiment R. I. L. A.
William H. Tanner. Sergeant in New York Chasseurs.
George M. Twitchell. Sergeant in 3d Regiment R. I. H. A.

ROLL OF THE REGIMENT.   215

Alfred Waldron. Wounded and taken prisoner in the battle of Bull Run, July 21, 1861. Released, May, 1862.
Charles W. Whipple. Private in 4th Regiment R. I. V.
Henry C. Wightman.
William J. Williams. Private in 1st Regiment R. I. C.
Allison A. Williams. Discharged May 9th.
John Wilson. Private in 1st Regiment R. I. C.
Augustus Young.
Francis H. Young.
Robert O. Young.

Commissary Department.

Coomer A. Easterbrook.
George H. Damon. Private 4th Regiment R. I. V.
John C. Brown. Corporal in 1st Regiment R. I. C.
John Luther Jr.
Benjamin F. Hiscox.

The nativities of this company are as follows: Rhode Island, 47; Massachusetts, 8; Connecticut, 7; Maine, 3; Vermont, 3; New York, 4; New Hampshire, 1; Pennsylvania, 1; Ohio, 1; Germany, 7; Ireland, 7; England, 3; Scotland, 1; Switzerland, 1; France, 1; Nova Scotia, 1; not returned, 17. Total, officers and men, 113.

Killed, 1; wounded, 2; taken prisoner, and since died, 1; wounded and taken prisoner, 1.

Average age, 26 years. Oldest man, 59; youngest, 18.
Average height, 5 feet, 7 inches.

This company has furnished for the war, 1 Captain, 3 Lieutenants, 17 Sergeants,* 12 corporals, and 28 Privates; to the navy of the United States, 2 Seamen.

---

* 1 Sergeant mortally wounded.

COMPANY I.

Henry C. Card, Captain. Captain in 9th Regiment R. I. V., (three months.)
William H. Chapman, First Lieutenant.
James Babcock, Second Lieutenant.
J. Clark Barber, Ensign. Lieutenant in 9th Regiment R. I. V., (three months).
Erastus W. Barber, First Sergeant.
James McDonald, Second Sergeant. Lieutenant in 9th Regiment R. I. V
Reuben S. Lamphear, Third Sergeant.
Henry R. Horton, Fourth Sergeant. Sergeant in 1st Regiment R. I. L. A.
Horace Swan, First Corporal.
Evan C. Burdick, Second Corporal.
Paul M. Barber, 2d, Third Corporal.
John F. Jencks, Fourth Corporal.
George P. Kenyon, Musician.
William Kenneth. Musician.
Isaac Allen. Private in 3d Regiment R. I. H. A.
Robert H. Andrews. Corporal in 1st Regiment R. I. L. A.
George P. Austin. Corporal in 5th Regiment R. I. V.
Horace G. Barber. Wounded in the battle of Bull Run July 21st, 1861.
L. A. Barber. Private in 4th Regiment R. I. V.
Thomas S. Barber. Discharged May 31st.
Uriah Baton. Private in 9th Regiment R. I. V.
William Baton.
Richard E. Barden. Lieutenant in 5th Regiment R. I. V. Afterwards discharged.
George W. Bennett. Private in 1st Regiment R. I. C.
Jeremiah A. Blaisdell.
Samuel Bliven.
George Braman. Discharged July 3d. Private in 1st Regiment R. I. L. A.

ROLL OF THE REGIMENT.

Amos L. Burdick. Private in 9th Regiment R. I. V., (three months.)
Albert H. Burdick. Mortally wounded at Bull Run July 21.
Alvin L. Card. Corporal in 4th Regiment R. I. V.
Patrick Casey. Private in 8th Regiment Conn. Vol.
Thomas N. Chapman. Private in 1st Regiment R. I. L. A.
Joshua Clark.
Joseph H. Clark. Corporal in 5th Regiment R. I. V
Edwin R. Cottrel. Private in 9th Regiment R. I. V
Daniel B. Cornell. Corporal in 1st Regiment R. I. L. A.
Elisha W Cross. Private in 1st Regiment R. I. L. A.
Nathan J. Crandall. Private in 9th Regiment R. I. V., three months).
John C. Crandall. Discharged May 31st.
Samuel C. Danforth. Killed in the battle of Bull Run, July 21.
Albert E. Denison.
William Dingavan. Sergeant in 3d Regiment R. I. H. A.
Joseph T. Dunham. Private in a New York Regiment.
Charles G. Ecclestone.
John Ecclestone.
Samuel R. Ecclestone.
James A. Edwards. Private in 9th Regiment R. I. V.
Walter H Ellard. Wounded at the battle of Bull Run, July 21st, 1861.
Lewis C. Fiske.
Theodore B. Floyd.
George C. Gardiner. Discharged June 9th.
Charles A. Graves.
Martin S. Greene. Discharged, June 9th. Farrier in 1st Regiment R. I. C.
Nelson Gibson. Sergeant in 4th Regiment R. I. V
Harris Havens.
William F. Hawkins. Private in 9th Regiment R. I. V.
Charles D. Holmes. Corporal in 3d Regiment R. I. H. A.
Frederic A. Hunt. Sergeant in 4th Regiment R. I. V.

APPENDIX D.

George H. Hull. Sergeant in 3d Regiment R. I. H. A.
Edgar W. Irish. Corporal in — Regiment R. I. V
Henry R. Jennings.
Andrew J. Keables.
Orren M. Keables. Discharged, July 3d.
Thomas H. Kelley.
Nathan W. Lewis.
Walter R. Lewis. Sergeant in 9th Regiment R. I. V.
William Lucas. Private in 8th Regiment Conn. V.
Andrew M. Morgan. Lieutenant in 8th Conn.
Henry E. Morgan. Lieutenant in 8th Conn.
George P. Nugent. Private in 9th Regiment R. I. V.
Charles H. Nichols. Discharged, June 15th.
Andrew Owens.
Austin A. Perkins. Private in 3d Regiment R. I. H. A.
James H. Perigo. Private in 9th Regiment R. I. V
Arnold Phillips.
George N. Phillips.
Job Phillips.
George A Place.
Israel A. Potter.
Henry H. Remington.
Joseph Richmond. Discharged July 3d. Private in 9th Regiment R. I. V
Lorenzo D. Richmond.
James C. Richardson.
James D. Roche. Lieutenant in 11th Conn.
Orson C. Rogers. — Regiment R. I.
Gilbert C. Sanders. Private in a New York Regiment.
Nathan H. Saunders. Private in 3d Regiment R. I. V.
Charles W Sheffield. Sergeant in 1st Regiment Conn. Cav.
Thomas D. Sheffield. Captain in 8th Conn.
William Sheep. Private in 3d Regiment R. I. V
Dudley F. Sisson. Private in 3d Regiment R. I. V
Peleg D. Sisson. Private in 9th Regiment R. I. V

ROLL OF THE REGIMENT. 219

Francis D. V. Sloan. Private in 8th Conn.
John H. Smith. Private in 8th Conn.
John H. D. Sprague. Wounded in the battle of Bull Run, July 21, 1861. Private in 8th Conn.
Henry Staplins. Private in 8th Conn.
David Sunderland.
Jeremiah Sullivan. Discharged May 31st. Sergeant in 3d Regiment R. I. H. A.
Avery Teft.
Benjamin R. Thurston.
John F. Trask. Wounded and taken prisoner in the battle of Bull Run July 21st. Released, May, 1862.
Harly Walker. Discharged June 15th.
John H. Weaver. Private in 4th Regiment R. I. V.
John W. Webster.
Roderick D. Whipple. Corporal in 1st Regiment R. I. H. A.
Charles P. Williams. Sergeant in 1st Regiment R. I. H. A.
Thomas S. Wright. Sergeant in 11th Regiment U. S. A. Promoted to Lieutenant, May 3d, 1862.

The nativities of this company were as follows: Rhode Island, 49; Connecticut, 21; New York, 8; Maine, 2; Vermont, 2; New Hampshire, 1; Massachusetts, 1; New Jersey, 1; Pennsylvania, 1; England, 5; Scotland, 2; Ireland, 2; not returned, 12. Total, officers and men, 107.

Killed, 1; mortally wounded, 1; wounded, 3; wounded and taken prisoner, 1.

Average age, 25 years. Oldest man, 42; youngest, 18.

Average height, 5 feet, 7 7-8 inches.

This company has furnished for the war, 1 Captain, 4 Lieutenants,* 9 Sergeants, 8 Corporals, 18 Privates, and 1 Farrier; and to the service for three months, 1 Captain, 2 Lieutenants, and 12 Privates.

---

* 1 Lieutenant discharged.

COMPANY K.

Peter Simpson, Jr., Captain.
Thomas Steere, First Lieutenant.
John A. Allen, Second Lieutenant. Major (Lieut.-Colonel) 4th Regiment R. I. V
George H. Grant, Ensign. Captain in 5th Regiment R. I. V.
Albert E. Greene, First Sergeant. Lieut. in 3d Regiment R. I. H. A.
John B. Bachelor, Second Sergeant. Sergeant in 3d Regiment R. I. H. A.
Henry C. Mowry, Third Sergeant. Mail Agent.
George W Green, Fourth Sergeant. Sergeant in 3d Regiment R. I. H. A.
Erastus S. Bartholomew, First Corporal. Appointed Sergeant, and promoted to be Lieutenant in 3d Regiment R. I. H. A., May 21, 1862. Mortally wounded in battle of James Island, June 16th, 1862. Died June 17th.
Waldo F. Slocomb, Second Corporal.
Edwin W Wheelock, Third Corporal.
Francello G. Jillson, Fourth Corporal. Lieutenant in 9th Reg't R. I. V (three months.)
Daniel H. Goff, Musician.
John J. Boyle, Musician. Drummer in 4th Regiment R. I. V.
William H. Ackley. Died in Hospital July 24th.
Almon Ballou.
George A. Black. Sergeant in 4th Regiment R. I. V
James Bloomingdale.
Amos Boyden. Sergeant in 5th Regiment R. I. V.
William C. Boyden, Jr.
Oscar L. Bradley.
George R. Buffum. Corporal in 4th Regiment R. I. V
Frank Caffrey.
John H. Carney. Artificer in 1st Regiment R. I. L. A.
Benjamin J. Carter. Discharged July 4th.

ROLL OF THE REGIMENT. 221

William L. Cates. Private in 3d Regiment R. I. H. A.
Dexter Clark.
George B. Clemence. Private in 4th Regiment R. I. V.
George Y. Coleman. Discharged July 9th.
Caleb W. Colvin. Corporal in 5th Regiment R. I. V.
James M. Colvin. Private in 24th Reg't Mass. Vols.
Foster M. Cook. Wagoner in 3d Regiment R. I. H. A.
Henry L. Cook.
Henry C. Davis. Died in Hospital, June 16th.
John J. Dixon. Discharged May 10th.
Barney J. Dodge.
Joseph Duprey. Sergeant in 4th Regiment R. I. V.
Daniel Farrar. Private in 3d Regiment R. I. H. A.
John Farrar. Corporal in 9th Regiment R. I. V (3 mos.)
Xavier D. Fisher. Private in 3d Regiment R. I. H. A.
Arlon T. Follett.
Alonzo M. Fuller. Sergeant in 3d Regiment R. I. H. A.
Hial C. Gore.
Asa R. Greene.
Charles C. Greene. Sergeant in 5th Regiment R. I. V.
William Guinness.
John Hackett. Sergeant in 3d Regiment R. I. H. A.
John W. Hallowell. Private in 3d Regiment R. I. H. A.
Joseph Harrop. Killed at the battle of Bull Run, July 21, 1862.
Charles M. Hayden.
John Hayward. Sergeant in 9th Regiment R. I. V. (3 mos.)
Edgar Hazleton. Private in 1st Regiment R. I. L. A.
George J. Hill. Sergeant in 3d Regiment R. I. H. A. Killed at Fort Pulaski, April 14th, 1862.
Gardiner H. Howe.
James B. Jackson.
Zachariah Jacobs. Wounded and taken prisoner at the battle of Bull Run, July 21, 1861.
Ethan A. Jencks. Lieutenant in 7th Regiment R. I. V

APPENDIX D.

Henry Jenerson. Corporal in 3d Regiment R. I. H. A.
Charles A. Joslin.
Andrew Jillson. Private in 4th Regiment R. I. V
Thomas Lord.
George Lovely.
Augustus Luther. Private in 3d Regiment R. I. H. A.
Henry Madden. Private in 3d Regiment R. I. H. A. Afterwards discharged.
George W. Mars.
Olney Marsh.
Matthew Martin.
Joseph N. Mason.
William McClure.
Patrick McGrath. Private in 1st Regiment R. I. L. A.
Orlando McIntyre. Discharged July 9th. Private in 15th Regiment Mass. Vols. Taken prisoner at Ball's Bluff. Released May, 1862.
Frank M. M. McKeirman. Discharged May 10th.
Hugh Melville. Killed in the battle of Bull Run, July 21st.
William Merchant.
Oliver Miett. Private in 3d Regiment R. I. H. A.
Henry C. Miller. Corporal in 4th Regiment R. I. V
Philip Miller. Private in 3d Regiment R. I. H. A.
John J. Murray. Corporal in 4th Regiment R. I. V.
Peter Munger. Private in 3d Regiment R. I. H. A.
George Nichols.
John M. Parker. Sergeant in 4th Regiment R. I. V.
William S. Partridge.
Horace H. Peirce. Private in 1st Regiment R. I. C.
Alonzo M. Pickering. Corporal in 5th Regiment R. I. V.
Matthew Quirk. Killed in the battle of Bull Run, July 21st.
Peter Riley.
Smith Robinson, Jr. Sergeant in 4th Regiment R. I. V.
Thomas W. Ryan. Private in 3d Regiment R. I. H. A.
John J. Sanborn.

Patrick Sheridan. Private in 4th Regiment R. I. V.
Christopher H. Shultz. Corporal in 1st Regiment R. I. C.
William H. H. Smith.
Lyman P. Southwick.
Nelson Spooner.
John H. Steere. Private in 1st Regiment R. I. C.
Daniel Sullivan. Private in 10th Reg't R. I. V. (3 mos.)
Hiram B. Tift.
Robert Thompson. Discharged July 9th.
Daniel Turner.
Nathan B. Vibbert. Private in 3d Regiment R. I. H. A.
Charles S. Watson. Captain in 9th Reg't R. I. V. (3 mos.)
Ferdinand L. Watson. Private in 4th Regiment R. I. V
Martin Welch.
Peter Wheelock.
Henry J. Whitaker. Lieutenant in 9th Reg't R. I. V (3 mos.)
Thomas E. White.
Leander White.
Alfred Wild. Sergeant in 5th Regiment R. I. V.
Robert L. Williams. Corporal in 1st Regiment R. I. L. A.
John Young.

The nativities of this company were as follows: Massachusetts, 35; Rhode Island, 24; Vermont, 8; Connecticut, 4; New York, 4; Maine, 3; New Hampshire, 1; England, 11; Ireland, 6; Canada, 2; Germany, 1; Saxony, 1; Switzerland, 1. Not returned, 9. Total, Officers and men, 110.

Killed, 3; taken prisoner, 1.

Average age, 25 years. Oldest man, 45. Youngest, 16.

Average height, 5 feet. 6⅞ inches.

This company has furnished for the war, 1 Major; 1 Captain; 3 Lieutenants; 12 Sergeants; 8 Corporals; 1 Artificer; 1 wagoner; 1 drummer, and 21 privates;* and for the service for three months, 1 Captain; 2 Lieutenants; 1 Sergeant, and 2 Privates.

---

*1 Private discharged.

APPENDIX D.

CARBINEERS.

A company of Carbineers, to act as skirmishers, was formed, by details from the other companies, and armed with the Burnside rifles.* On the ninth of June it was organized as a separate corps, and its place in the line of march was in front of the column. Its officers were appointed as follows:

Francis W Goddard, commissioned as Captain.
Walter B. Manton, commissioned as Lieutenant.
John B. Campbell, of Company A, Sergeant.
George O. Gorton, of Company C, Sergeant.
Robert H. Deming, of Company D, Sergeant.
Louis T. Hall, of Company G, Sergeant.
Peleg E. Bryant, of Company B, Sergeant.

The Company numbered seventy-three privates, but its members messed, quartered, and were paid with their respective companies. Consequently no roll was preserved, and I am unable to record their names.

James Allen, of the Light Battery, and William H. Helme, of Company C, were authorized to act as aeronauts, in connection with the movements of the regiment. Previous to the advance into Virginia, they were detailed, with a corps of assistants, to serve under the direction of General McDowell, for the purpose of making balloon reconnoisances of the enemy's positions. Ample materials were furnished them, and valuable results would doubtless have been accomplished, had their experiment proved successful. But, by accident, the two balloons in their possession were rendered useless, and thus the

---

* Lieut. Charles E. Patterson, of the 4th Infantry, U. S. A., was detailed to act as drill-master of the Carbineers, before their organization as a separate corps. One morning, he did not appear, as usual. We soon ascertained the reason. We learned, with regret, that he had deserted to the rebel army; for he was an amiable, gentlemanly officer, of excellent bearing and address. He was dismissed from the service, June 6, 1861. After his departure. Lieut. Sisson, Paymaster of the Regiment, did efficient service in drilling the company.

commanding General was deprived of information which would have been of great advantage on the day of battle.

NATIVITIES.

The nativities of the entire Regiment were as follows:— Rhode Island, 612; Massachusetts, 187; New York, 59; Connecticut, 57; Maine, 31; Vermont 19; New Hampshire, 16; Pennsylvania, 7; New Jersey, 6; Maryland, 2; Illinois, 2; Indiana, 1; Michigan, 1; Ohio, 1; Virginia, 1; District of Columbia, 1; Ireland, 50; England, 46; Germany, 29; Scotland, 12; Nova Scotia, 3; Prussia, 3; Switzerland, 3; Canada, 2; France, 2; Bavaria, 2; Cuba, 1; Holland, 1; Saxony, 1; Wirtemberg, 2; not returned, 140.

Whole number, including Officers, Band and Battery, 1,300. Average age, 25 1-4 years. Average height, 5 feet 7 1-4 inches.

CASUALTIES.

The casualties of the Regiment were, as follows: Killed, 12; wounded, 33; taken prisoner 22, of whom 12 were wounded; mortally wounded and taken prisoner, 6; missing, 1; died in service, 5. Total casualties, 79. Discharged and resigned, 61.

OCCUPATIONS OF THE MEMBERS OF THE REGIMENT·

FIELD AND STAFF.

Physicians, 5; Manufacturers, 3; Accountants, 2; Clergymen, 2; Druggist, 1; Civil Engineer, 1; Lawyer, 1; Railroad Treasurer, 1; not returned, 2.

NON-COMMISSIONED STAFF.

Clerk, 1; Druggist, 1; Jeweller, 1; Lawyer, 1; Merchant, 1; Plumber, 1; not returned, 2.

APPENDIX D.

REGIMENTAL BAND.

Musicians, 8; Jewellers, 7; Painters, 2; Engraver, 1; Farmer, 1; Instrument Maker, 1; Moulder, 1; Photographer, 1; Plater, 1; Silversmith, 1.

LIGHT BATTERY.

Jewellers, 24; Clerks, 17; Carpenters, 8; Machinists, 8; Moulders, 6; Blacksmiths, 3; Drivers, 3; Hostlers, 3; Laborers, 3; Printers, 3; Shoemakers, 3; Chemists, 2; Gasfitters, 2; Gentlemen, 2; Farmers, 2; Hatters, 2; Masons, 2; Musicians, 2; Painters, 2; Sailors, 2; Silversmiths, 2; Spinners, 2; Students, 2; Tanners, 2; Teamsters, 2; Aeronaut, 1; Banker, 1; Bank Cashier, 1; Barkeeper, 1; Box Maker, 1; Brakeman, 1; Butcher, 1; Carriage Maker, 1; Cigar Maker, 1; Coachman, 1; Cooper, 1; Cotton Broker, 1; Cutler, 1; Dentist, 1; Die Sinker, 1; Engineer, 1; Gilder, 1; Grocer, 1; Harness Maker, 1; Insurance Agent, 1; Lapidary, 1; Lumber Dealer, 1; Merchant, 1; Miller, 1; Police, 1; Soldier, 1; Tin-worker, 1; Tradesman, 1; Veterinary Surgeon, 1; not returned, 8.

COMPANY A.

Jewellers, 20; Clerks, 7 Machinists, 6; Accountants, 5; Carpenters, 4; Masons, 4; Painters, 4; Moulders, 3; Students, 3; Tobacconists, 3; Druggists, 2; Police, 2; Printers, 2; Baker, 1; Bagmaker, 1; Bootmaker, 1; Carriage Maker, 1; Carver, 1; Colorer, 1; Currier, 1; Die Sinker, 1; Driver, 1; Engine Builder, 1; Engraver, 1; File Cutter, 1; Grocer, 1; Hostler, 1; Laborer, 1; Lawyer, 1; Marble Cutter, 1; Newspaper Correspondent, 1; Operator, 1; Photographer, 1; Sailmaker, 1; Sailor, 1; Salesman, 1; Silversmith, 1; Tin-worker, 1; Wood engraver, 1; not returned, 18.

COMPANY B.

Jewellers, 17; Machinists, 15; Moulders, 8; Carpenters, 6; Painters, 6; Laborers, 4; Blacksmiths 3; Clerks, 3; Farmers,

ROLL OF THE REGIMENT. 227

3; Dresser Tenders, 2; Puddlers, 2; Sailors, 2; Tailors, 2; Teamsters, 2; Weavers, 2; Barkeeper, 1; Butcher, 1; Cabinet Maker, 1; Chaser, 1; Coppersmith, 1; Gasfitter, 1; Gilder, 1; Lawyer, 1; Mason, 1; Nailer, 1; Pattern maker, 1; Printer, 1; Roofer, 1; Shoemaker, 1; Silversmith, 1; Stonecutter, 1; Tin worker, 1; Trader, 1; Varnisher, 1; not returned, 12.

COMPANY C.

Jewellers, 25; Clerks, 22; Students, 7; Machinists, 5; Engravers, 4; Marble Cutters, 4; Lawyers, 3; Merchants, 3 Rubber Manufacturers, 3; Tin workers, 3; Carpenters, 2; Grocers, 2; Moulders, 2; Silversmiths, 2; Cabinet Maker, 1; Carriage Maker. 1; Dentist, 1; Diesinker, 1; Engine turner, 1; Gasfitter, 1; Gentleman, 1; Lapidary, 1; Manufacturer, 1; Mechanic, 1; Painter, 1; Physician, 1; Police, 1; Sailor, 1; Sashmaker, 1; Trader, 1; Tradesman, 1; Watch-caser, 1; not returned, 9.

COMPANY D.

Jewellers, 31; Clerks, 14; Accountants, 4; Moulders, 4; Students, 4; Carpenters, 3; Dentists, 3; Artists, 2; Farmers, 2; Grocers, 2; Machinists, 2; Silversmiths, 2; Bottler, 1; Butcher, 1; Cabinet Maker, 1; Carriage Maker, 1; Designer, 1; Druggist, 1; Engineer, 1; Gasfitter, 1; Gentleman, 1; Lumberman, 1; Manufacturer, 1; Mason, 1; Mechanic, 1; Merchant, 1; Nailer, 1; Painter, 1; Photographer, 1; Printer, 1; Rubber Manufacturer, 1; Sailor, 1; Shoemaker, 1; Stove Manufacturer, 1; Tailor, 1; Tobacconist, 1; Turner, 1; Upholsterer, 1; Watchmaker, 1; not returned, 17.

COMPANY E.

Jewellers, 23; Carpenters, 11; Clerks, 9; Machinists, 9; Painters, 9; Laborers, 5; Blacksmith, 3; Farmers, 3; Moulders, 2; Shoemakers, 2; Artist, 1; Barber, 1; Butcher, 1; Chaser, 1; Chemist, 1; Clock Maker, 1; Cloth Inspector, 1;

228   APPENDIX D.

Confectioner, 1 ; Currier, 1 ; Daguerrean, 1 ; Draughtsman, 1 ; Dresser tender, 1 ; Dyer, 1 ; Engineer, 1 ; Fireman, 1 ; Gasfitter, 1 ; Manufacturer, 1 ; Mule Spinner, 1 ; Pedler, 1 ; Roofer, 1 ; Sailor, 1 ; Spinner, 1 ; Student, 1 ; Teamster, 1 ; Wheelwright, 1 ; Not returned, 4.

COMPANY F.

Carpenters, 14 ; Painters, 11 ; Sailors, 7 ; Clerks, 5 ; Farmers, 5 ; Masons, 4 ; Tinworkers, 4; Blacksmiths, 3 ; Bootmakers, 3 ; Gentlemen, 3 ; Sailmakers, 3 ; Butchers, 2 ; Carriagemakers, 2 ; Coopers, 2 ; Laborers, 2 ; Machinists, 2 ; Merchants, 2 ; Plumbers, 2 ; Teamsters, 2 ; Bonnet Maker, 1 ; Cabinetmaker, 1 ; Calico printer, 1 ; Coal dealer, 1 ; Druggist, 1 ; Engineer, 1 ; Express messenger, 1 ; Fisherman, 1 ; Gasfitter, 1 ; Harness maker, 1 ; Lawyer, 1 ; Master builder, 1 ; Moulder, 1 ; Music teacher, 1 ; Operative 1 ; Printer, 1 ; Provision dealer, 1 : Shoemaker, 1 ; Soap boiler, 1 ; Tailor, 1 ; Not returned, 10.

COMPANY G.

Jewellers, 15 ; Carpenters, 11 ; Painters, 8 ; Machinists, 6 ; Laborers, 5 ; Shoemakers, 5 ; Weavers, 4 ; Gasfitters, 3 ; Farmers, 3 ; Moulders, 3 ; Sailors, 3 ; Silversmiths, 3 ; Accountants, 2 ; Butchers, 2 ; Clerks, 2 ; Die sinkers, 2 ; Drivers, 2 ; Actor, 1 ; Baker, 1 ; Barber, 1 ; Blacksmith, 1 ; Bookseller, 1 ; Brass founder, 1 ; Broom maker, 1 ; Carder, 1 ; Carriage trimmer, 1 ; Colorer, 1 ; Engineer, 1 ; Engraver, 1 ; Fireman, 1 ; Ice man, 1 ; Mason, 1 ; Piecer, 1 ; Printer, 1 ; Shoe dealer, 1 ; Spinner, 1 ; Stone cutter, 1 ; Tailor, 1 ; Teamster, 1 ; Tin worker, 1 ; Trader, 1 ; Not returned 10.

COMPANY H.

Sailors, 11 ; Jewellers, 10 ; Laborers, 8 ; Painters, 6 ; Carpenters, 5 ; Moulders, 5 ; Spinners, 4 ; Blacksmiths, 3 ; Butchers, 2 ; Clerks, 2 ; Machinists, 2 ; Merchants, 2 ; Shoemakers, 2 ; Tailors, 2 ; Accountant, 1 ; Barber, 1 ; Bookbinder, 1 ;

ROLL OF THE REGIMENT. 229

Bootmaker, 1; Box maker, 1; Brass finisher, 1; Brush maker, 1; Cabinet maker, 1; Calico printer, 1; Carriage maker, 1; Currier, 1; Die sinker, 1; Dress tender, 1; Engineer, 1; Express messenger, 1; Farrier, 1; Grocer, 1; Horse Jockey, 1; Hostler, 1; Lithographer, 1; Mason, 1; Musician, 1; Nailer, 1; Physician, 1; Plumber, 1; Sash maker, 1; Servant, 1; Tin worker, 1; Tool maker, 1; Weaver, 1; Not returned, 19.

COMPANY I.

Spinners, 14; Farmers, 13; Machinists, 13; Laborers, 7; Carpenters, 6; Carders, 4; Dresser tenders, 4; Weavers, 4; Blacksmiths, 3; Moulders, 3; Sailors, 3; Stone cutters, 3; Teamsters, 3; Accountant, 1; Butcher, 1; Colorer, 1; Daguerrean, 1; Dentist, 1: Doormaker, 1; Engineer, 1; Finisher, 1; Fisherman, 1; Harness maker, 1; Mason, 1; Merchant, 1; Teacher, 1; Tin worker, 1; Not returned, 13.

COMPANY K.

Laborers, 17; Spinners, 15; Shoemakers, 8; Weavers, 8; Carpenters, 6; Dresser tenders, 5; Farmers, 5; Clerks, 4; Scythe makers, 3; Blacksmiths, 2; Harness makers, 2; Hostlers, 2; Lawyers, 2; Machinists, 2; Tin workers, 2; Carder, 1; Dentist, 1; Driver, 1; Druggist, 1; Manufacturer, 1; Marble worker, 1; Mason, 1; Merchant, 1; Painter, 1; Printer, 1; Sailor, 1; Shoedealer, 1; Soap manufacturer, 1; Stone cutter, 1; Stone mason, 1; Tailor, 1; Woolsorter, 1: Not returned, 10.

RECAPITULATION.

Jewellers, 173; Clerks, 86; Carpenters, 76; Machinists, 70; Laborers, 52; Painters, 51; Moulders, 38; Farmers, 37; Spinners, 37; Sailors, 33; Shoemakers, 23; Blacksmiths, 21; Weavers, 19; Students, 17; Masons, 16; Accountants, 15; Tin workers, 15; Dresser tenders, 13; Merchants, 12; Silversmiths, 12; Butchers, 11; Musicians, 11; Teamsters, 11; Gas-

APPENDIX D.

fitters, 10; Lawyers, 10; Printers. 10; Tailors, 8; Carriage makers, 7; Dentists, 7; Drivers, 7; Druggists, 7; Engineers, 7; Engravers, 7; Gentlemen, 7; Grocers, 7; Hostlers, 7; Manufacturers, 7; Physicians, 7; Carders, 6; Die sinkers, 6; Marble cutters, 6; Stone cutters, 6; Bootmakers, 5; Cabinet makers, 5; Harness makers, 5; Police, 4; Plumbers, 4; Rubber manufacturers, 4; Sail makers, 4; Tobacconists, 4; Artists, 3; Barbers, 3; Chemists, 3; Colorers, 3; Coopers, 3; Curriers, 3; Nailers, 3; Photographers, 3; Scythe makers, 3; Traders, 3; Bakers, 2; Barkeepers, 2; Box makers, 2; Calico printers, 2; Chasers, 2; Clergymen, 2; Daguerreans, 2; Express messengers, 2; Firemen, 2; Fishermen, 2; Gilders, 2; Hatters, 2; Lapidaries, 2; Mechanics, 2; Puddlers, 2; Roofers, 2; Sashmakers, 2; Shoe dealers, 2; Tanners, 2; Tradesmen, 2; Actor, 1; Aeronaut, 1; Bagmaker, 1; Banker, 1; Bank cashier, 1; Bonnet maker, 1; Bookbinder, 1; Bookseller, 1; Bottler, 1; Brakeman, 1; Brass finisher, 1; Brass founder, 1; Broom maker, 1; Brushmaker, 1; Carriage trimmer, 1; Carver, 1; Cigar maker, 1; Civil Engineer, 1; Clock maker, 1; Cloth Inspector, 1; Coachman, 1; Coal dealer, 1; Confectioner, 1; Coppersmith, 1; Cotton broker, 1; Cutler, 1; Designer, 1; Door maker, 1; Draftsman, 1; Dyer, 1; Engine builder, 1; Engine turner, 1; Farrier, 1; Filecutter, 1; Finisher, 1; Horse jockey, 1; Ice man, 1; Instrument maker, 1; Insurance agent, 1; Lithographer, 1; Lumber man, 1; Lumber dealer, 1; Master builder, 1; Miller, 1; Mule spinner, 1; Music teacher, 1; Newspaper correspondent, 1; Operative, 1; Operator, 1; Pattern maker, 1; Pedler, 1; Piecer, 1; Plater, 1; Provision dealer, 1; Railroad treasurer, 1; Salesman, 1; Servant, 1; Soap boiler, 1; Soap manufacturer, 1; Soldier, 1; Stone mason, 1; Stove manufacturer, 1; Teacher, 1; Tool maker, 1; Turner, 1; Upholsterer, 1; Varnisher, 1; Veterinary surgeon, 1; Watch caser, 1; Watchmaker, 1; Wheelwright, 1; Wood engraver, 1; Wool sorter, 1. Not returned, 134.

RECAPITULATION OF OFFICERS AND OTHERS FURNISHED FOR THE WAR.

The Regiment has furnished for the war, 1 Major General; 2 Brigade Surgeons; 1 Assistant Surgeon; 1 Superintendent of Hospital; 1 Chaplain; 3 Colonels; 1 Lieutenant Colonel of the Staff; 4 Lieutenant Colonels; 2 Majors; 2 Captains of the Staff; 21 Captains of the Line; 2 Adjutants; 3 Quartermasters; 69 Lieutenants; 1 Bandmaster; 4 Sergeant Majors; 130 Sergeants; 47 Corporals; 4 Artificers; 2 Buglers; 3 Hospital Stewards; 1 Assistant Government Agent; 1 Clerk to Major General; 1 Clerk to Commissary; 1 Farrier; 1 Aeronaut; 4 Scouts; 1 Sutler; 1 Saddler; 1 Drummer; 3 Wagoners; 2 Hostlers; 1 Private in band; and 158 Privates:—to the army of the United States, 1 Captain; 4 Lieutenants, and 1 Assistant Paymaster:—to the Navy of the United States, 1 Lieutenant; 1 Acting Master; 7 Master's Mates; 1 Lieutenant in Marine Corps; 1 Lieutenant in Naval Brigade; 1 Captain's Clerk; 8 Seamen; 1 Landsman; 1 Bandmaster, 4 Privates in Band and 2 Watchmen at Naval School; 1 Laborer at Navy Yard:—and to the service for three months, 1 Colonel; 1 Lieutenant Colonel; 1 Major; 2 Adjutants; 9 Captains; 14 Lieutenants; 1 Sergeant Major; 18 Sergeants; 12 Corporals; 1 Farrier; and 33 Privates.

NOTE. 1 Colonel, 1 Captain, 1 Lieutenant, 2 Sergeants, and 1 Private killed—1 Captain, A D C; 1 Captain; 3 Lieutenants, 1 Sergeant Major, 1 Scout, and 1 Sutler resigned—1 Chaplain, 1 Lieutenant, 1 Sergeant, 2 Privates, and 1 Seaman, discharged, and 1 Sergeant, 1 Corporal and 1 Private deserted. In the three months service, 1 Lieutenant Colonel, 1 Major, 1 Adjutant, 1 Captain, resigned.

APPENDIX E.

FINAL PARADE.

The Light Battery, in the temporary command of Lieut. Remington, reached Providence, on Wednesday, July 31, and its members were welcomed in Railroad Hall, by their friends, on Thursday morning, August 1. They were addressed by Hon. Thomas A. Jenckes, as follows:

Lieutenant Remington and Soldiers:—In behalf of the citizens of Providence, I give to you their greeting. They had hoped to have seen you on Sunday, with the regiment, that you might have felt and known the grandeur and sincerity of the welcome which Rhode Island gives to her returning sons. But you were detained by duty. As you were the first to leave us, so you are the last to return to us. The alacrity with which you rushed to the field will ever be the joy and pride of your lives, as it is the gratification of your fellow-citizens. I well remember the chagrin of the New Yorkers when the echoes of their harbor were broken by a battery from Rhode Island, and the stillness of their streets by the march of a regiment from Massachusetts, while as yet the energies of their great city had but a single body of men in the field, in answer to the requisition of the President.

From the time you left us, you have not ceased to be the object of our most anxious interest. We have been with you, in spirit, in your long and tedious marches. We have observed you transferred from post to post, from commander to commander, from this tedious duty to that harrassing toil. We have marked your privations. We have suffered with you in your disappointments. We know of your wearisome marches and countermarches, in the presence of a wiley foe. We know that it is not your fault that you have not covered yourselves with glory on the field of battle. You are not to blame for the want of capacity or of patriotism in the generals who were placed over you.

Soldiers of the Marine Battery, we, as citizens of the State of Rhode Island, are proud of you; as citizens of the United States of America, we are grateful for your services; and now, to you, as soldiers of the republic, about to return and resume your duties as citizens, we, on behalf of all our fellow-citizens, tender our most cordial welcome.

He was followed by Col. Burnside in a brief speech, which was most enthusiastically received. He regretted the separation between them at the seat of war, and assured them of his confidence and warm regard. He thought they would have been better satisfied to have remained and taken part in the battle which had so distinguished the regiments from Rhode Island. Wherever they might meet hereafter, the kindest feelings of his heart would be with them. At the conclusion of breakfast, the marines were escorted back to their armory by the Infantry, who in turn repaired to their armory and were dismissed.

The regiment spent the remainder of the day in drill and parade. At the close, the companies, (with the exception of F, I, and K, which had been mustered out of the service in the afternoon), were drawn up in Exchange Place, when Adjutant Merriman read the following general order.:

HEADQUARTERS 1ST REG't R. I. D. M.
Providence, Aug. 1, 1861.

General Orders No. 29.

The Colonel commanding the First Regiment Rhode Island Detached Militia, in bidding farewell to the soldiers who, for the past three months, have been under his command, takes this occasion to express his satisfaction with the conduct of the officers and men composing the regiment during their season of military service. The brief period for which they were enrolled has afforded an opportunity for witnessing all the aspects of a long campaign. Life in camp, peaceful parades, fatiguing marches, a bloody battle, alternate victory and defeat have been their portion. Yet, in whatever position they have been placed, they have creditably sustained the honor of the State that sent them forth. They have won for themselves an enviable reputation abroad, and the certain regard of their fellow citizens at home.

Upon the very outset of their career, they were subjected to the disagreeable necessity of a tedious journey through an unfriendly territory. Direct communication with Washington, through the accustomed channels, had been interrupted, and the regiment was compelled to go by sea from New York to Annapolis. A march of twenty-two miles lay before them. Though unaccustomed to duty of this kind, both officers and men accepted it with cheerfulness and engaged in it with alacrity. The bivouac, the continued march, the arrival at Washington amid the greetings of the citizens, attested the high sense of duty which characterized this movement. When the regiment went into quarters at the Patent Office, it was with the consciousness of fidelity in the performance of a perilous task; the feeling of satisfaction that the point of danger had been reached, and a readiness to accept whatever the future might have in store.

The life in camp bore the same characteristics. Cheerfulness in obedience to orders, promptness in response to the call of duty, patient endurance of discipline and hardship, were evidences of the character of men who were willing to do well for the country, and sacrifice much for the cause in which they were engaged. The favor with which the regiment was regarded by all classes of the citizens of Washington, amply testifies to the strong hold which it had secured upon the public sympathy and confidence.

The regiment had been enrolled for the defence of Washington against the plots of treason and the invasion of a rebellious force. Yet, when the order came for a distant expedition, to attack the entrenchments of the rebels at Harper's Ferry, the men of Rhode Island, true to their instincts of loyalty, did not hesitate to obey. Transferred to another command, they were still obedient to their sense of duty. The toils and fatigues of the expedition were suffered without a murmur. The march from Greencastle to Williamsport, exposed to the hottest rays of a midsummer sun ; the long, almost unprecedented march from Williamsport to Frederick City, were tests of endurance bravely met and borne, and the regiment returned to its camp, with even a better reputation than it had before sustained.

The term of enlistment was fast drawing to a close. Three months, in fact, had well nigh expired since the regiment had left its home, when the advance into Virginia was ordered. Still faithful to its first grand impulse, the 1st Rhode Island Regiment joined its comrades in the ranks of the great army of the Union, and went forward to battle. The silent midnight preparation and departure, the long, fatiguing march before the dawn and through the morning, the hotly contested fight, when the two Rhode Island regiments stood shoulder to shoulder, like brothers and friends, the temporary victory, the final defeat and disastrous retreat are now familiar to the public mind. The Colonel commanding does not think it necessary to dwell upon these subjects. They are now matters of history. He thinks it sufficient to say to the regiment and to the public, that in all these transactions and events, Rhode Island has no cause to be ashamed of her sons. He desires to declare, in the most emphatic terms, his approbation of the bearing and behaviour of his whole command. He wishes also to express his admiration of the gallant conduct of the 2d Rhode Island Regiment while under his temporary direction. He remembers, with heartfelt sorrow, the painful, yet glorious death of Slocum, Ballou, Tower, Smith, Prescott, and others, in both our regiments, who fell upon the battlefield and by the wayside. Their bravery commends them to the grateful esteem of an appreciative public, and their memory will be cherished in the hearts of all Rhode Island men.

It was with real regret that the Colonel commanding, a few weeks ago, parted with the 1st Battery of Light Artillery, and it was with the most cordial feeling that, yesterday, he welcomed its return. He regards with an honest pride the effective service, which the officers and men composing this company have rendered to the regiment, the State, and the country. Always ready at the call of duty, prompt and brave in the field, they have done credit to themselves and honor to their fellow-citizens. Though not permitted to participate in the recent dangers and duties of the battlefield, they have yet been active upon other scenes of service, and the Colonel commanding takes this opportunity to thank them for their efficiency, fidelity and courage.

In relinquishing his position, the Colonel commanding would express his thanks to his Excellency the Governor of the State of Rhode Island, for timely aid and counsel, for an unwearied support, and for a cordial co-operation with every plan and purpose; to the people of the State for their kind and too indulgent appreciation of his services, and for their repeated and unforgetful acts of kindness; to the officers of the field and staff, for their judicious and faithful observance of his wishes; and to all the officers of the line and the men of the regiment, for the respect and affection which they have always manifested towards him. A kind Providence has smiled upon our ways, and helped us in our works, and we return thanks to Almighty God for his favor towards us in preserving us amid dangers and disease, and returning us in safety to our homes. May the same

Divine love encompass us in all our future hours, and at last give unto us an eternal peace.

By order of
A. E. BURNSIDE, Col. Com'g.
C. H. MERRIMAN, Adjutant.

The address was received with nine hearty cheers.

The Chaplain of the regiment, Rev. Mr. Woodbury, then read a portion of the Scriptures, and closed with prayer. Chaplain Quinn then made a short and effective address. Mr. Woodbury pronounced the benediction, the band played Old Hundred, and the regiment was dismissed.

FINAL ADDRESS OF COLONEL BURNSIDE.

At a special session of the General Assembly of the State of Rhode Island, held in August, 1861, resolutions of thanks to Col. Burnside, and the regiment, were adopted by that body and transmitted to Col. B., by the Governor, in compliance with the vote of the Assembly. Col. Burnside thereupon issued the following address:

PROVIDENCE, Aug. 22, 1862.
To the Officers and Soldiers of the First Regiment Rhode-Island Detached Militia.

COMRADES:—I have great pleasure in transmitting to you, through the public press, the resolutions which were passed, at the recent session of the General Assembly of our State, and communicated to me by his Excellency the Governor, in acknowledgment of your services in the camp and the field. I feel that you have well deserved this honor. By your ready compliance with my wishes, and your prompt obedience to my orders, you have won my sincerest esteem. By your brave endurance of fatigue, hardship and peril, and by your gallantry upon the battle field, you have gained the grateful regard of your fellow-citizens. The State, acting through its proper authorities, recognizes the value of your services, and places among its archives its estimate of your worth. It is gratifying for me to mention that his Excellency the Governor, has uniformly expressed these opinions respecting your bearing, and has given his hearty concurrence to my arrangements for you in the camp, upon the march, and in the dispositions of battle.

I address these few words to you upon the eve of my departure for a distant scene of duty. I shall bear with me from this State, the most kindly remembrances of the generosity and confidence of my fellow-citizens. Whatever may be my future fortunes, and wherever my future career may be led, I shall always consider it as among the highest privileges of my life, that I have had the honor to command the FIRST REGIMENT RHODE ISLAND DETACHED MILITIA.

"RESOLUTION of thanks to Ambrose E. Burnside, late Colonel of First Regiment Rhode Island Detached Militia.

Resolved, That the thanks of the General Assembly be, and the same are hereby, presented to Ambrose E. Burnside, late Colonel of the First Regiment Rhode Island Detached Militia, for the prompt and patriotic manner in which he tendered his services to his adopted State at the call of our country for soldiers to protect its capital and sustain its government under the national constitution; for his assiduous care and skillful conduct of the soldiers of this State placed under his charge; and for the skill and generalship displayed by him upon the field of battle, which, we are pleased to learn, has been recognized and rewarded by the national government.

Resolved, That, through Col. Burnside, we also tender the thanks of the General Assembly to the officers and soldiers of his command, who volunteered so promptly for their country's service.

Resolved, That the General Assembly would be gratified to learn that the regiments raised by this State, for the service of the national government, were to be placed under the immediate command of General Ambrose E. Burnside.

Resolved, That His Excellency the Governor be requested to cause a copy of these resolutions to be communicated to Colonel Burnside, and that Colonel Burnside be requested to communicate the same to the officers and soldiers late under his command.

APPENDIX F.

THE REGIMENTAL COLORS.

Previous to our departure from Rhode Island, a beautiful national flag, made of silk and ornamented with gold fringe and tassels, was presented to the Regiment by the ladies of Providence.

The correspondence in connection with this presentation sufficiently explains itself.

To the First Regiment Rhode Island Volunteers,
from the Ladies of Providence:

With this banner, Rhode Island places her honor in your hands. May God protect you in your noble course. God save the Union.

Providence, April 19th, 1861.

Col. Burnside made the following reply:

HEADQUARTERS RHODE ISLAND MILITIA,
Providence, April 19th, 1861.

To the Ladies of Providence:

I know the gallant men I carry away will prove themselves worthy of the beautiful banner presented to them by you.

We are fully impressed with the fact, that we take with us your most fervent prayers, and we shall constantly feel that

your eyes are upon us. God grant that we may yet see the Union out of danger. Bidding you an affectionate farewell, and thanking you, in behalf of my command, for your kindness,
I am ever yours,
A. E. BURNSIDE,
Col. 1st Regiment R. I. D. M.

That flag was carried through the campaign, and received at the battle of Bull Run the marks of eleven bullets. The color sergeant and one of the guard were wounded, when it was taken and defended by private Hamilton, of Company F, who brought it from the field. It is now in possession of the State. Other flags were afterwards presented to the Regiment, of which I am enabled to append a brief and grateful notice.

After the commencement of the war, the citizens of Rhode Island resident in California prepared two sets of colors to be presented to the 1st and 2d Regiments of their native State. Subsequent to the return of the First Regiment these flags were forwarded to Rhode Island. Those designed for the 2d Regiment were sent to the authorities of the State; those for the 1st Regiment, to the Mayor of the city of Newport, to be placed in the custody of the color company, " F," of that city. The flags, one of Rhode Island, as a regimental flag, and one of the United States, were among the most beautiful specimens of the kind. They were of silk, embroidered with silver and silver mounted. They bore the inscription:—" Presented by Rhode Islanders resident in California to the First Regiment Rhode Island Detached Militia." Hon. Wm. H. Cranston, Mayor of Newport, has kindly furnished me with a copy of the following communication which accompanied the gift.

SAN FRANCISCO, CALIFORNIA,
August, 30th, 1861.

His Honor William H. Cranston, Mayor of the City of Newport:

SIR:—At a meeting of the natives and citizens of Rhode Island now residents of California, we, the undersigned, were appointed a Committee to forward to your Honor a set of Regimental Colors for the First Regiment, R. I. D. M, to be by you presented to them in person, as a token of our esteem and admiration for the prompt, noble and efficient response made by them to the patriotic call of our Country to fight for Constitutional liberty, and for the brave, honorable and veteran-like manner in which they have performed their duties.

Very respectfully, your obedient servants,

WILLIAM SHERMAN,
E. P. PECKHAM,
JAS. N. OLNEY,
B. H. RANDOLPH,
C. V S. GIBBS.

The following address, signed by the donors, also accompanied the standard:

SAN FRANCISCO, August, 1861.

To the Officers and soldiers of the
First Rhode Island Regiment, D. M.:

BROTHERS:—Although we are distant from you by some thousands of miles, we are still loyal American citizens, and are neither unmindful of the honor of our birthplace, nor indifferent to your service and gallantry in behalf of the common cause. Our hearts were stirred with enthusiam when we read here of the promptness with which our native State offered her thoroughly appointed Regiments, in the critical hour, for the protection of the Capital. They swelled with sacred pride when we followed the story of Rhode Island's fidelity and discipline on the retreat from Manassas, and saw

APPENDIX F.

Rhode Island names gleaming brightly through the mists that obscure that page in the annals of our righteous war. We pledge to you our sympathy, and confess our admiration, and offer our gratitude in the Flag and Standard which will accompany this letter. They are the cordial gift of the sons of Rhode Island, residents in California.

The stars and stripes are our colors and emblems by the Pacific, and will be while her surf beats against the cliffs of the Golden Gate.

The anchor is the emblem of our firm devotion to the cause for which you have periled your lives, and are ready still to devote your treasure and your blood. We know that you will accept them with a full response to the spirit in which they are offered.

Think of the breadth and majesty of the country for which you have unsheathed your swords when you receive these Colors. If you take them into battle, make a new vow under them to the *Constitution*, which diffuses blessings from the coasts of New England to the shores of Oregon. Pledge yourselves more deeply against the treason that would destroy it. And may the God of justice and of battles help and protect you in our common struggle for Order, Liberty and Law.

N. Porter,	W. R. Bourne,
B. H. Randolph,	G. W. Gibbs,
A. J. Gladding,	J. B. Newton,
H. L. Davis,	L. H. Knowles,
G. M. Almy,	Stephen Smith,
E. C. Angell,	F. J. B. Thompson,
Wm. Sherman,	E. B. Gibbs,
E. F. Childs,	J. G. Chappell,
Wm. Norris,	A. M. Humphrey,
A. B. Cranston,	O. W Spencer,
R. J. Stevens,	E. W. Burr,
H. D. Cogswell,	E. P. Peckham,
Chas. E. Hinckley,	C. V. S. Gibbs,
J. F. McKenzie,	Wm. A. Bateman,
B. C. Harris, Jr.,	Wm. H. Bovee,

THE REGIMENTAL COLORS.

J. N. Olney,
F. J. Lippitt,
Jas. R. Richards,
R. M. Sherman,
Chas. E. Gibbs,
H. Pierson,
J. P. Vernon,
J. H. Sherman,
L. H. Newton,
B. S. Proctor,
J. H. Spooner,
B. T. Chase,
H. A. Davis,
E. F. Northam,
R. B. Gray,
Smith Brown,
M. Smith,
Isaac Gibb,
Wm. A. Church,
Jas. Burdick,
J. D. Burdick,
B. W Arnold,
S. W Burdick,
G. N. Briggs,
E. Culver,
Edwin Harris,
Jas. E. Boyce,
C. C. Baker,
Jas. Elton,
Wm. Roberts,
J. Hammond,
B. Southorth,
Geo. T. Pearce,
W. H Montgomery,
F. A. Gibbs,
J. Hammond,
C. Remington,
S. T. Watson,
Wm. F. Osborn,
F. A. Olney,
G. H. Pettus,
J. A. Brown,
C. Burr,

R. B. Williams,
E. V. Hathaway,
E. J. Blanding,
J. D. Coulter,
H. B. Angell,
A. W. Harris,
Jas. H. Demarest,
F. M. Hoxie,
Arnold Peirce,
S. A. Wood,
Chas. Clark,
B. M. Claflin,
P. T. Smith,
C. Williston,
Geo. D. Weaver,
A. W. Pitts,
A. B. Brown,
E. P. Bucklin,
S. C. Harding
D. W K. Bokee,
R. P. Handy,
Wm. Woodward,
Wm. B. Hubbard,
E. M. Chapin,
S. C. Welborn,
S. S. Nickerson,
C. H. Lapham,
Charles E. Knowles,
J. Simmons,
A. R. Dyer,
W F Allyn,
J. C. Caswell,
W. Williston,
Thos. Corwin,
Wm. Horr,
B. Claflin,
A. F. Dyer,
S. Whipple,
B. C Allen,
J. A. Salsbury,
Wm. B. Kendrick,
Chas. S. Leux,
J. Emerson,

APPENDIX F.

Chas. Woodward,	S. T. Randall,
H. T. Burr,	Abel Thornton,
J. B. Taylor,	J. N. Olney, Jr.,
J. L. Peck,	E. N. Burlin,
M. B. Almy,	R. Card.
Robert Ray,	H. A. Kelley,
Wm. J. Pettus,	H. B. Porter,
C. H. Dexter,	G. S. Hall,
C. Hutchinson,	Abel Wade,
Jno. N. Swan,	D. Tafft,
D. Sherman,	N. J. Pettiplace,
D. T. Mathewson,	J. R. Congdon,
E. R. Harris,	J. R. Matheson,
L. B. Arnold,	B. S. Thornton,
Robert Cairns,	Francis Pearce,
M. R. Thurber,	A. J. Almy,
G. Robinson,	J. R. Wilkinson,
Ira Merriman,	A. T. Lawton,
W. Smith,	P. A. Cook,
E. W. Barber,	Jas. E. Boyce,
H. Pettiplace,	Jas. F. Angell,
Wm. R. Keach,	J. H. N. Gardner,
E. P. Lindsey,	S. Hendrickson,
J. Mathewson,	Chas. Keeley,
E. P. Clark,	Jno. J. Cushing,
H. Carrison,	N. Crowell,
W C. Briggs,	Henry Hull,
Chas. Hopps,	F J. B. Thompson,
O. D. Sherman,	Stephen H. Smith,

R. Sweet.

On Tuesday, Oct. 29th, 1861, the flags previously received were presented, with appropriate ceremonies, by Mayor Cranston to General Burnside, who in turn presented them to the members of Company F, which was paraded for their reception. Mayor Cranston delivered a very earnest and eloquent address on the occasion, concluding as follows:

"Accept this offering—our unconquered and unconquerable national flag—and this State Standard, the emblem of freedom for more than two hundred years—the patriotic and cheerful gift of Rhode Islanders in the Eden of the Pacific to you their brothers in the Eden of the Atlantic. Guard them sacredly and well—carefully preserve and affectionately cherish them; if necessary, lay down your lives in their defence against foreign invasion or domestic insurrection, and your reward will be the gratitude of all future generations of honest and loyal men on earth—the approbation of God, and eternal felicity in that new Paradise, where there will neither be wars or rumors of wars, and where the King of Kings and the Prince of Peace will reign Supreme forever."

General Burnside responded in a neat and effective address. After acknowledging the kindness of the patriotic Californians, he turned to the members of Company F, and said:

"With you, Company F, I leave these colors. For their proper keeping I need give you no charge. You have been tried, and have indeed been found not wanting. Take them, accept them as a part of the history of the 1st Rhode Island Regiment and as a part of the history of your own gallant State, and as an emblem of the glory of your dearly loved country. Love the one flag and revere the other. Many dark hours we have already passed through, and many more are yet to be undergone. But let no man of us all falter as to the success of this glorious cause. In all our work, however dangerous or arduous, we shall be followed by the prayers of loved friends at home, and of the true and loyal of all our country, and of the good and true of every land. The Great God above may chasten us in His wisdom, but rest assured He will never forsake us in His justice.

To you, Mr. Mayor, I render my sincere thanks for your kind words of me. They are indeed precious to me. The words of commendation which have been spoken of my conduct by my approving fellow-citizens, are my highest reward. And as to Company F, I have no fears but they will do as they have done before—their whole duty. Better soldiers never trod the soil of this or any other land. Not a man of them failed to execute my orders to the letter. Never soldiers did their duty—their whole duty, more promptly or gallantly."

Then taking one flag and handing it to Ensign Hamilton, and the other to Ensign DeBlois, he added:

"Take these beautiful flags, Company F. Take them and keep them. You have the well-earned right to keep them. Twice was your own flag stricken down in the field of battle, and then a third man from your ranks seized it, and it was borne aloft in safety from the field, though pierced with many a bullet."

Then turning to the Mayor, he added:

" And, in conclusion, allow me to thank you and all concerned in this presentation, for these beautiful gifts to Rhode Island's First and gallant Regiment."

At the conclusion of General Burnside's remarks, Captain Charles E. Lawton came upon the stage, and in behalf of the Regiment, offered a series of resolutions. These were principally in answer to the address of presentation which was sent from California.

Whereas, We have this day received from Rhode Islanders residing in California, a set of splendid Colors—the American Flag and the Standard of Rhode Island,—being as they have kindly said, a testimonial of their appreciation of our loyalty to the Constitution and the Union, as well as the promptness with which we responded to the call of the Chief Magistrate of the United States to defend the Capital at the time of its most imminent danger: therefore,

Resolved, That we fully appreciate the loyalty and generosity of our brother Rhode Islanders residing in California, and that in gratefully accepting these Colors, we assure our absent friends that we will guard them carefully and sacredly, and protect them, on all occasions, with the same earnest spirit with which we endeavored to discharge our duty to our Country, during the period of our enlistment in the volunteer service of the United States.

Resolved, That we return our sincere thanks to our liberal donors for these Colors, which shall never be disgraced in our hands; and that we will on all occasions strive to merit the praise that they have bestowed upon, and the confidence that they have reposed in us; and that while many of our comrades have again enlisted in the service of their Country, we are also ready, whenever it is necessary, to encounter the enemy, and discharge our whole duty for the preservation of the Union.

Resolved, That we trust that we may always be entitled to be called as true sons of Rhode Island and as sincere patriots, as are our brothers on the Golden shores of the Pacific, who, though long absent from home, still fondly love this home of their early years, and are firmly devoted to the Union of these States which has always offered a hospitable home to the oppressed of all nations.

Resolved, That Gen. A. E. Burnside, our late beloved Colonel, be requested to send a copy of these Resolutions to the Committee of the donors in California.

At the conclusion of their reading, Gen. Burnside stepped forward and put them to vote to Company F, who represented, in this case, the whole Regiment. They were unanimously adopted.

The ceremonies ended by a parade of Company F and the Old Guard Newport Artillery, through the principal streets of the city, displaying the flags which had been presented. The colors are now in possession of the Mayor of Newport.

APPENDIX G.

MISCELLANEOUS.

The law of the State, passed by the General Assembly, April 17th, 1861, for the furnishing of the quota of Rhode Island for the militia required by the President of the United States, and under the provisions of which the First Regiment and Battery were enlisted, was as follows:

Whereas, the President of the United States has, by proclamation dated April 15, A. D. 1861, called forth the militia of several States of the Union, to the aggregate number of seventy-five thousand, and has assigned one regiment as the quota of this State:

It is enacted by the General Assembly as follows:

Section 1. The commander-in-chief is hereby authorized to raise by detailing from the chartered companies of this State, or by voluntary enlistment, or by draft, so many regiments, battalions, or companies of troops for service within or without this State, and to arm and equip the same, as in his opinion the public service may require, or as have been, or shall be called for by requisition from the President of the United States; the same to be organized as prescribed by the act of Congress entitled "An act more effectually to provide for the national defence, by establishing an uniform militia throughout the United States," approved May 8, A. D. 1792.

Sec. 2. The Governor shall appoint the regimental officers; the Colonel shall enlist a Band, subject to the approval of the Governor.

Sec. 3. As soon as the troops so raised are formed into companies, each company shall elect one captain, one lieutenant, one ensign, four sergeants, four corporals, one drummer, one fifer, by the major vote of such company, the commissioned officers of said company to be approved and commissioned by the Governor; and their relative rank shall be determined by lot.

Sec. 4. The non-commissioned staff, and the non-commissioned officers of companies shall receive warrants from the colonel, and vacancies shall be filled, if of a company officer, by an election by the company; if of a field officer, by the Governor; if of an officer of the regimental staff, by the colonel.

Sec. 5. All commissions issued in pursuance of this act shall remain in force from the time the engagements are taken thereon, and as long as the persons holding the same shall remain in the service of the United States; and if any officer of the militia of this State now in commission shall accept a commission under this act, he shall, at the end of his service, be restored to the same position and rank held by him when he accepted such position.

Sec. 6. All officers, non-commissioned officers and privates, raised in pursuance of this act, shall receive the same pay, allowances and emoluments as are now allowed to those of the same grade in the army of the United States, from the date of their commissions or enrollments to the time they shall be mustered into the service of the United States, during which period they shall be subject to the orders of the commander-in-chief; and in addition to said pay, the non-commissioned officers, privates and musicians shall receive, as bounty, the sum of twelve dollars per month during their service, which shall be paid monthly in advance, upon their orders, by the Paymaster General.

Sec. 7. The troops which may be raised under this act shall be armed, clothed, equipped, provisioned and furnished as may be necessary and proper for service, at the expense of this State, until mustered into the service of the United States; and the Governor is hereby authorized to draw on the General Treasurer for all sums necessary to defray the expenses incurred under this act; and the General Treasurer is hereby directed to pay the same out of any money in the treasury not otherwise appropriated.

Sec. 8. This act shall take effect from and after the passage thereof.

The following resolution and act were passed on Thursday, April 18th, 1861, after which the General Assembly adjourned:

Resolved, That the Paymaster General be, and he hereby is, directed to pay to the order of each of the commissioned officers of the regiment of troops which has been raised, and is about to depart in answer to the requisition of the President of the United States, a sum of money equal to one month's pay, according to the laws of the United States.

It is enacted by the General Assembly as follows:

Section 1. In addition to the officers authorized by the act to which this is in addition, there shall be a second surgeon's mate in the staff of each regiment, to be appointed by the Governor, and one second lieutenant to each company, who shall be elected by such company. Such officers shall be commissioned, and shall be entitled to the pay and allowances provided by said act for surgeons' mate and lieutenant.

Section 2. The Governor is authorized to commission such officers for any company of artillery as he may deem necessary, who shall be entitled to the pay and allowances of officers of like grades provided by the act to which this is in addition.

Section 3. This act shall take effect from and after its passage.

All the above were introduced by W. P. Sheffield, Esq., of Newport. In this connection, I may be allowed to state, that the Regiment was greatly indebted, at different times during the summer, to Messrs. Sheffield, Brown, Robinson and Brayton, of Rhode Island; Hon. C. H. Van Wyck, of New York, and E. H. Rollins, of New Hampshire, of the U. S. House of Representatives, and Messrs. Anthony and Simmons, of the U. S. Senate, for franking and supplies of stationery.

THE EXPENDITURES OF THE REGIMENT.

The Quartermaster General of the State, in making report of the expenses of the State for carrying on the war, under date of January 27, 1862, makes the following statement relative to the First Regiment and Battery:

MISCELLANEOUS.

Supplies furnished the First Rhode Island Regiment and First Battery Light Artillery:

Clothing	$24,525 25
Blankets	6,024 12
Hats and Caps	3,603 56
Shoes	2,689 96
Camp Equipage	4,050 51
Equipments	10,412 49
Subsistence	73,589 80
Quarters	1,986 36
Local and Special Transportation	3,125 77
Transportation	40,077 90
Arms	6,262 18
Ammunition	1,507 86
Contingent Expenses	3,461 14
Medical Department	1,486 73
Horses	17,670 00
Harnesses and Horse Equipments	2,067 42
Forage	823 74
Wagons	2,202 50
Stationery and Blank books	507 96
Materials for Battery	684 89
	$206,760 14
To this amount are to be added,	
Bounty to officers 1st Regiment and Battery	7,336 15
" men " "	44,232 00
Total Expenses	$258,328 29

The explanation is added: "The excess of expenditure in arming, transporting and subsisting the First Regiment and Battery over that of any other, must be attributed, in part, to the hurried manner of their organization, and in part to the great outlay for subsistence, (the United States not being in condition to furnish it,) while they were in Washington." In justice to the Regiment it should also be stated, that a portion of the subsistence account should be charged to the Second Regiment, inasmuch as the two regiments, while encamped together, were furnished from the same commissary stores.

Considerable deductions are to be made from the items, "equipments," "arms," "horses," "harness and horse equipments" and "wagons," as the largest portion of these was returned to the State. Immediately previous to the departure of the regiment from Washington, all the muskets in its possession, (which were of a superior quality, being "Minie rifled,") were exchanged, piece for piece, for the "smooth bore" muskets of the Second Regiment, and these latter were brought home and deposited with the State authorities. A considerable amount of "clothing"—"hats and caps," "blankets" and "shoes,"—were turned over to the Second Regiment, when the First Regiment left Washington, and all the guns, horses, and equipments of the First Battery were transferred to the Second. It is no more than proper, also, to state that the allowance for clothing and transportation, (in the latter case amounting to twenty-three days's pay, a sum of $15,000) was relinquished by the officers and men in behalf of the State. In judging of the expenditures for the regiment, the above facts are to be considered.

THE UNION ARMY AT THE BATTLE OF BULL RUN.

FIRST DIVISION.

Brigadier General Daniel Tyler, Connecticut Militia, commanding.

First Brigade.

Colonel E. D. Keyes, Eleventh Infantry, U. S. A., commanding.

First Regiment Connecticut Volunteers.
Second Regiment Connecticut Volunteers.
Third Regiment Connecticut Volunteers.
Second Regiment Maine Volunteers.
Captain Varian's Battery of New York Eighth Regiment.
Company B, Second Cavalry, U. S. A.

Second Brigade.

Brig. Gen. R. Schenck, Ohio Volunteers, commanding.
First Regiment Ohio Volunteers.
Second Regiment Ohio Volunteers.
Second Regiment New York Volunteers.
Company E, Second Artillery, light battery.

MISCELLANEOUS. 253

Third Brigade.

Colonel William T. Sherman, Thirteenth Infantry, U. S. A. commanding.
Sixty-ninth Regiment New York Militia.
Seventy-ninth Regiment New York Militia.
Thirteenth Regiment New York Volunteers.
Second Regiment Wisconsin Volunteers.
Company E, Third Artillery, U. S. A., light battery.

Fourth Brigade.

Colonel J. B. Richardson, Michigan volunteers, commanding.
Second Regiment, Michigan Volunteers.
Third Regiment Michigan Volunteers.
First Regiment Massachusetts Volunteers.
Twelfth Regiment New York Volunteers,

SECOND DIVISION.

Colonel David Hunter, Third Cavalry, U. S. A., commanding

First Brigade.

Colonel Andrew Porter, Sixteenth Infantry, U. S. A., commanding.
Battalion of Infantry, Second, Third and Eighth Regiments, U. S. A.
Eighth Regiment New York Militia.
Fourteenth Regiment New York Militia.
Squadron Second Cavalry, U. S. A., Companies G and L.
Company Fifth Artillery, U. S. A., light battery.

Second Brigade.

Colonel A. E. Burnside, Rhode Island Volunteers, commanding.
First Regiment Rhode Island Detached Militia.
Second Regiment Rhode Island Volunteers.
Seventy-first Regiment New York Militia.
Second Regiment New Hampshire Volunteers.
Battery of light artillery, Second Rhode Island Regiment.

THIRD DIVISION.

Colonel S. P. Heintzelman, Seventeenth Infantry, U. S. A., commanding.

22

First Brigade.

Colonel W. B. Franklin, Twelfth Infantry, U. S. A., commanding.
Fourth Regiment Pennsylvania Militia.*
Fifth Regiment Massachusetts Militia.
First Regiment Minnesota Volunteers.
Company E, Second Cavalry, U. S. A.
Company I, First Artillery, U. S. A., light battery.

Second Brigade.

Colonel O. B. Wilcox, Michigan Volunteers, commanding.
First Regiment Michigan Volunteers.
Eleventh Regiment New York Volunteers.
Company D, Second Artillery, U. S. A., light battery.

Third Brigade.

Colonel O. O. Howard, Maine Volunteers, commanding.
Third Regiment Maine Volunteers.
Fourth Regiment Maine Volunteers.
Fifth Regiment Maine Volunteers.
Second Regiment Vermont Volunteers.

RESERVE—FOURTH DIVISION.

Brigadier General Theo. Runyon, New Jersey Militia, commanding.
First Regiment New Jersey Militia, three months volunteers.
Second Regiment New Jersey Militia, three months volunteers.
Third Regiment New Jersey Militia, three months volunteers.
Fourth Regiment New Jersey Militia, three months volunteers.
First Regiment New Jersey Militia, three years volunteers.
Second Regiment New Jersey Militia, three years volunteers.
Third Regiment New Jersey Militia, three years volunteers.

FIFTH DIVISION.

Colonel D. S. Miles, Second Infantry, U. S. A., commanding.

First Brigade.

Colonel Blenker, New York Volunteers, commanding.

---

*Left Centreville on the morning of July 21, for Washington.

Eighth Regiment New York Volunteers.
Twenty-ninth Regiment New York Volunteers.
Garibaldi Guard.
Twenty-fourth Regiment Pennsylvania Volunteers.

Second Brigade.

Colonel Davies, New York volunteers, commanding.
Sixteenth Regiment New York Volunteers.
Eighteenth Regiment New York Volunteers.
Thirty-first Regiment New York Volunteers.
Thirty-Second Regiment New York Volunteers.
Company G, Second Artillery, U. S. A., light battery.

General McDowell's Staff consisted of the following gentlemen:

Captain James B. Fry, U. S. A., Assistant Adjutant General
Lieutenant H. W. Kingsbury, U. S. A., Aide de Camp.
Major Clarence S. Brown, New York State Militia, Aide de Camp.
Major James S. Wadsworth, New York State Militia, Aide de Camp.
Major W H. Wood, U. S. A., Inspector General.
Major J. G. Barnard, U S. A Engineer.
Lieutenant F E. Prime, U. S. A., Engineer.
Captain A. W Whipple, U. S. A., Topographical Engineer.
Lieutenant Henry L. Abbott, U. S. A., Topographical Engineer.
Lieutenant Handimand S. Putman, U. S. A., Topographical Engineer.
Captain O H. Tillinghast, U S. A., Assistant Quartermaster.
Captain H. F. Clark, U. S. A., Commissary.
Surgeon W S. King, U. S. A.
Assistant Surgeon, David L. Magruder, U. S. A.

THE REBEL FORCES AT THE BATTLE OF BULL RUN.

FIRST DIVISION, AT UNION MILLS.

First Brigade.

Brigadier General Richard S. Ewell, commanding.
Four Regiments, supposed to be
Fifth Regiment Alabama Volunteers, Colonel Rhodes.
Sixth Regiment Alabama Volunteers, Colonel Siebels.
Thirteenth Regiment Alabama Volunteers, Lieut. Colonel O'Hara.
Twelfth Regiment Mississippi Volunteers, Colonel Griffith.

Second Brigade.

Brigadier General Theophilus P. Holmes, commanding.
Second Regiment Tennessee Volunteers.
First Regiment Arkansas Volunteers.
Battery of Artillery, 6 pieces, Captain Lindsey Walker.
Company of Cavalry, Captain Scott.

SECOND DIVISION, ON THE LEFT OF THE FIRST DIVISION.

First Brigade.

Brigadier General David R. Jones, commanding.
Fifth Regiment South Carolina Volunteers, Colonel Jenkins.
Eighteenth Regiment Mississippi Volunteers, and three other Regiments, with
Two Batteries of Artillery, eight pieces, Captains Albertis and Stanwood.

Second Brigade.

Colonel —— Early, commanding.
Seventh Regiment Virginia Volunteers, Col. Kemper.
Seventh Regiment Louisiana Volunteers, Colonel Hay.
Thirteenth Regiment Mississippi Volunteers, Colonel Barkesdale.

THIRD DIVISION, AT BLACKBURN'S AND MITCHELL'S FORDS.

First Brigade.

Brigadier General Longstreet, commanding.
First Regiment Virginia Volunteers, Major Skinner.
Eleventh Regiment Virginia Volunteers, Colonel Garland.

Twenty-fourth Regiment Virginia Volunteers, Lieut. Colonel Hairston.
Seventeenth Regiment Virginia Volunteers, Colonel Corse.
Fifth Regiment North Carolina Volunteers. Lieut. Colonel Jones.
One Battery of Artillery, Colonel Pendleton.
One Company of Cavalry, Captain Whitehead.

Second Brigade.

Brigadier General T. J. Jackson, commanding.
Fourth Regiment Virginia Volunteers, Colonel Preston.
Fifth Regiment Virginia Volunteers, Colonel Harper.
Second Regiment Virginia Volunteers, Colonel Allen.
Twenty-seventh Regiment Virginia Volunteers, Lieut. Colonel Echols.
Thirty-third Regiment Virginia Volunteers, Colonel Cummings.

FOURTH DIVISION, IN THE REAR OF THE FORDS AND STONE BRIDGE AND ON TURNPIKE.

First Brigade.

Brigadier General Bonham, commanding.
Second Regiment South Carolina Volunteers, Colonel Kershaw.
Eighth Regiment South Carolina Volunteers, Colonel Cash.
Third Regiment South Carolina Volunteers, Colonel Williams.
Seventh Regiment South Carolina Volunteers, Colonel Bacon.
Eleventh Regiment North Carolina Volunteers, Colonel Kirkland.
Eighth Regiment Louisiana Volunteers, (six companies).
Two Batteries, 1 section of Artillery, Captains Shields and Kemper, and Lieut. Garnett.
Three Companies of Cavalry.

Second Brigade.

[Between Stone Bridge and Sudley.]
Brigadier General Barnard E. Bee, commanding.
Second Regiment Mississippi Volunteers, Colonel Falkner.
Fourth Regiment Alabama Volunteers, Colonel E. J. Jones.
Sixth Regiment North Carolina Volunteers, Colonel Fisher, joined at noon.

Eleventh Regiment Mississippi Volunteers.
One Battery of Artillery, 4 pieces, Captain J. B. Imboden.
One Battery of Artillery, two companies, 13 pieces, Major Walton.

Third Brigade.

Colonel Bartow, commanding.
Seventh Regiment Georgia Volunteers, Colonel Gartrel.
Eighth Regiment Georgia Volunteers.

FIFTH DIVISION, IN REAR OF STONE BRIDGE, TURNPIKE AND SUDLEY.

First Brigade.

Brigadier General P St. G. Cocke, commanding.
Nineteenth Regiment Virginia Volunteers, Lieut. Colonel Strange.
Eighteenth Regiment Virginia Volunteers, Colonel Withers.
Eighth Regiment Virginia Volunteers, (seven companies).
Forty-ninth Regiment Virginia Volunteers, (three companies), Colonel W Smith.
Twenty-eighth Regiment Virginia Volunteers, Col, Preston.
Hampton Legion.
One Battery of Artillery, Captain Rogers.
Two companies of Cavalry.

Second Brigade.

Brigadier General E. K. Smith, commanding.—[Who was shot, and succeeded by Colonel Arnold Elzey.]
Third Regiment Tennessee Volunteers, Colonel Vaughn.
First Regiment Maryland Volunteers, Colonel Stewart.
Tenth Regiment Virginia Volunteers, Colonel Gibbons.
One Battery of Artillery, (four pieces), Lieutenant Beckwith.

Third Brigade.
[At Sudley.]

Colonel Evans, commanding.
Fourth Regiment South Carolina Volunteers, Colonel Sloan.
One Battalion of Louisiana Volunteers, Major Wheat.
One Section of Artillery, Lieutenant Leftwitch.

MISCELLANEOUS. 259

Besides these forces, known to be present in the battle, or near the scene of action, there were in different parts of the field, Stuart's Cavalry ; 2 pieces of Artillery, under Lieutenant Stanard, 1 Battery, 4 pieces, under Captain Latham, and 1 Battery, 4 pieces, under Captain Heaton ; 1 Brigade of Infantry under Colonel Wilcox and 1 Regiment of Infantry, under Colonel Hill. All these troops were engaged, with the exception of Ewell's and Wilcox's Brigades. I have prepared the above statement from General Beauregard's official report. Other troops were on the rail roads leading to Manassas and arrived there on the night of July 21, and two or three successive days. There was a considerable force at Manassas Junction, holding the entrenchments for the rebels to fall back upon, if defeated.

ADDENDA TO APPENDIX C. AND D.

GEORGE CARPENTER, of Company D., was born in Seekonk, Mass., in the year 1832. He was a comb maker by occupation, but for several years past he had paid considerable attention to the study of the fine arts, in which he had shown decided manifestations of taste and skill. He enlisted in the regiment immediately upon its formation, and, throughout the campaign bore himself as a most exemplary man and a brave and high spirited soldier. He was wounded in the battle of Bull Run, July 21, 1861, but returned with the regiment to Washington, and afterwards to his home in Seekonk. Upon his recovery he was again induced to enter the service under Capt. N W Brown, who had been appointed Colonel of the 3d Regiment. Mr. Carpenter was commissioned as Lieutenant Oct. 9, 1861, and received the appointment of Quartermaster. He continued faithfully to perform the duties of this office until stricken by disease, which proved fatal. He died at Fort Seward, Bay Point, S. C. June 28, 1862. He was a young man of the finest qualities of character, and his memory is cherished by his surviving comrades as that of an honorable man, a faithful friend, and a fearless soldier.

DANIEL A. BOSS, of Co. F, was born in Newport, in the year 1841. He passed through the campaign of the first regiment creditably to himself, and upon the formation of the 4th Regiment, he decided to follow his old commander, Capt. Tew, once more to the field. He went with his regiment to North Carolina, and contracted there a disease which terminated his life at Beaufort, some time in June, 1862.

CHRISTOPHER C. RHODES was a member of Company G, in which he enlisted at the beginning of the war. He returned with the regiment, afterwards became ill, and died at Boston, Mass., July 28, 1862, aged 31 years.

Page 164. "Daniel L. Arnold," should be placed under "Company H."

The corrections in Appendix D, are made mostly from information obtained since the former sheets passed through the press.

Page 181. James F. Davison has been promoted to corporal.
Page 183. In casualties, read "wounded, taken prisoner and since died," 1.
Page 191. Lewis Richmond has been promoted to Lieut. Colonel.
Page 192. James O. Swan has been promoted to Com. Sergeant.
Page 193. Col. N. W Brown's resignation was not accepted by Gen. Hunter, commander of the Department of the South, as Col. B.'s services were considered too valuable to be dispensed with, and he consequently remains in command of the Third Regiment.
Page 194. George Carpenter died at Fort Seward, S. C., June, 28, 1862.
Page 209. Chris'r. C. Rhodes, died at Boston, Mass., July 28, 1862.
Page 218. Henry H. Remington, died at Providence, Aug. 28, 1861. "William Sheep," should read "William Sherp."
Pages 218 and 219. "3d Regiment, R. I. V." and "1st Regiment, R. I. H. A.," should read "3d Regiment R. I. H. A."
Page 219. At bottom, read "20 privates, and "10 privates" for "18 privates" and "12 privates." Add "To the Army of the United States, 1 Lieutenant."
Page 220. Strike out—("Lieut. Colonel")—after "John A. Allen."
Page 223. Nathan B. Vibbert is sergeant in 3d Regiment, R. I. H. A. Robert J. Williams has deserted. In casualties, add, "Died in service 2." In note, add 1 Lieutenant, 1 Sergeant killed, 1 Corporal deserted.
Page 225. In casualties, add, "sick, taken prisoner and died 1; disabled in service, 2. Total 82."

www.ingramcontent.com/pod-product-compliance
Lightning Source LLC
Chambersburg PA
CBHW031954230426
43672CB00010B/2148